How to Do Everything
Everything

BlackBerry® Storm2™

Joli Ballew

New York Chicago San Francisco Lisbon
London Madrid Mexico City Milan New Delhi
San Juan Seoul Singapore Sydney Toronto

The McGraw·Hill Companies

Cataloging-in-Publication Data is on file with the Library of Congress

McGraw-Hill books are available at special quantity discounts to use as premiums and sales promotions, or for use in corporate training programs. To contact a representative, please e-mail us at bulksales@mcgraw-hill.com.

How to Do Everything: BlackBerry® Storm2™

1234567890   WFR WFR   109876543210

ISBN   978-0-07-170332-1
MHID   0-07-170332-2

Sponsoring Editor
Megg Morin

Editorial Supervisor
Patty Mon

Project Manager
Harleen Chopra,
Glyph International

Acquisitions Coordinator
Meghan Riley

Technical Editor
Bonnie Cha,
Senior CNET Editor

Copy Editor
Margaret Berson

Proofreader
Susie Elkind

Indexer
Ted Laux

Production Supervisor
Jim Kussow

Composition
Glyph International

Illustration
Glyph International

Art Director, Cover
Jeff Weeks

Cover Designer
Jeff Weeks

For Dad, who at 89 years young, continually marvels at what these tiny phones can do.

About the Author

Joli Ballew is a technical author, technology trainer, community college instructor, and self-proclaimed "gadget expert," residing in Dallas, Texas. She holds several certifications including MCSE, MCTS, and MCDST. Joli has written over three dozen books on technologies ranging from Photoshop to operating systems to phones, and her work has been published in over ten languages.

In addition to writing and teaching, Joli works as a network administrator and web designer for North Texas Graphics, writes web pages for Microsoft, and writes articles for various online communities, including BrightHub. In her free time, she enjoys golfing, yard work, exercising at the local gym, and teaching her cats, Pico and Lucy, tricks.

Joli welcomes all correspondence and can be contacted via e-mail at Joli_Ballew@hotmail.com.

About the Technical Editor

Bonnie Cha is a senior editor for CNET.com, covering smartphones, and was also the technical editor for *How to Do Everything: Palm Pre*. Bonnie recently moved back to the East Coast after spending ten years in California, and when she's not testing the latest gadgets, you can find her exploring her new neighborhood in New York or looking for new surf spots.

Contents

vi Contents

Acknowledgments

I've written three *How to Do Everything* books, and have worked with just about everyone at McGraw-Hill. Each person involved in a book plays an important role, and I'm always amazed how complex the process actually is. While I only put words on paper, the editors, project managers, coordinators, proofreaders, supervisors, composers, and artists turn the words into a book I can hold in my hands and be proud of. The people who worked directly with me on this book include Roger Stewart, Megg Morin, Bonnie Cha, Meghan Riley, Patty Mon, and Jim Kussow, and I'd like to thank them for all their hard work.

Book writing takes a bit of family support too, and I'd like to thank mine for sticking by me through the months that I'm overworked, and the various times when I'm not. I miss my Mom, who passed away in 2009, and I am very proud of Dad for trudging through this difficult time with a smile on his face and faith in his heart. Faith is a good thing, and provides hope, security, and sanctuary for those who can find it.

Finally, I'd like to thank my agent, Neil Salkind, who continues to surprise me with his talents, tact, personal support, and connections, and how he goes out of his way to keep me busy. He's a great friend and my biggest fan, and I appreciate him.

Introduction

Congratulations on the purchase of your new BlackBerry Storm2. You're going to be amazed at how versatile this little device is, how many ways you can use it to stay in touch with others, and how many "apps" are available for you to play and work with. You'll love GPS, texting, adding participants to a phone conversation, and taking video footage, complete with a flash, too!

In order to help you get the most from your BlackBerry, you'll want to explore all aspects of it. That's why, in this book, we'll start with the seemingly simple (making phone calls), and work our way up to more exciting things, like using applications, downloading ring tones, transferring music from your computer, syncing photos, connecting with Wi-Fi, traveling with BlackBerry Maps, and geotagging with GPS. You'll even learn how to tether your phone to your laptop, should you ever need to.

Without further ado then, let's get started. Here's what you'll learn in this book:

Chapter 1, "Getting Started," helps get you through the setup process, learn the parts of the BlackBerry screen and case, send and receive phone calls, set up and get your voice mail, add contacts, place a voice-activated call, and set up a Bluetooth headset. When you're finished with this chapter you'll know all there is to know about the "phone" part of the BlackBerry Storm2.

Chapter 2, "Explore Messaging," introduces you to the various messaging options for your BlackBerry, including BlackBerry Messenger, SMS and MMS, and third-party programs like Windows Messenger. Whichever option you prefer, you'll learn how to send and receive messages, both text and pictures, and how to manage the messages you receive.

Chapter 3, "Use Your Camera," instructs you on using the media card that came preinstalled in your BlackBerry Storm2, and how to take pictures using the camera and store those pictures to the card. You'll learn to how to use zoom and flash, show the pictures you've taken, and even create a slideshow of images. Finally, you'll learn how to shoot video using the video camera, and view what you've recorded.

Chapter 4, "Change Your BlackBerry's Look and Feel," walks you through personalizing your BlackBerry. You'll learn how to create a welcome message, apply a password, and configure other security-related tasks, as well as how to change the desktop wallpaper, reposition and hide Home screen icons, change what the convenience keys do, and even add your own AutoText entries. You'll explore accessories too, like headphones and ear buds. Your BlackBerry Storm2 should stand out, and this chapter is all about making yours stand out the most!

Chapter 5, "Download Ring Tones, Wallpaper, and Themes," shows you one way to get ring tones, wallpaper, and themes onto your BlackBerry Storm2. In this chapter, you'll learn how to navigate to the official BlackBerry Mobile web site (using only your phone) to access media you can download. After locating the web site, you'll create a bookmark for it and then browse the site and download and apply tones, wallpapers, and themes. Most of the items discussed in this chapter are free, so there's no need to set up a PayPal account or visit App World. This is a good place to start if you only want a new ring tone or wallpaper, and you want to get it from an official BlackBerry web site.

Chapter 6, "Use BlackBerry App World," shows you how to install App World, get a PayPal account, and purchase media including games, business applications, instant messaging and social networking applications, themes, utilities, and more. You'll learn how to access and read application reviews, how to download and pay for applications, and how to write your own reviews of the applications you own. There are thousands of applications to choose from, so set some time aside for browsing.

Chapter 7, "Set Up and Use E-mail," helps you learn the differences among e-mail options including BlackBerry e-mail, third-party e-mail applications, corporate e-mail, and personal POP3 or HTTP-based e-mail. You'll set up an e-mail account, read, forward, and reply to e-mail, delete and manage e-mail, and even add attachments to e-mails you send.

Chapter 8, "Explore Advanced E-mail Options," you'll learn how to log on to the BlackBerry Internet Service (BIS) web site and discover additional ways to manage your e-mail. You can create filters to limit what e-mail arrives on your phone, create, edit and add a signature to outgoing e-mails, check spelling, request a read receipt, and edit e-mail settings, among other things.

Chapter 9, "Explore Internet and Browser Basics," shows you how to surf the web right from your phone. You'll visit web pages, search with keywords, zoom to a page, click links, and copy and send Internet addresses. You'll also learn to set a Home page, play media on a page, add a bookmark and manage bookmarks you keep, create bookmark subfolders, and configure browser options, including browser push.

Chapter 10, "Use Wi-Fi," teaches you how to connect your BlackBerry Storm2 to a free Wi-Fi hotspot and to your own wireless network. Wi-Fi is often faster than the service you get through your provider, and can offer better performance. After you've made a few connections you'll learn how to manage your Wi-Fi network list, read connection indicators, and turn on and off Wi-Fi when applicable to save battery power.

Chapter 11, "Getting Around with Maps and GPS," teaches you how to use BlackBerry Maps, a free application that incurs no monthly fees, to locate yourself on a map and get directions to a destination. You can use BlackBerry Maps and GPS to locate businesses, specific addresses, or even types of places like coffee shops or libraries. BlackBerry Maps is only text-based, though, and does not offer voice directions. If you want something more sophisticated, you have options, though, and they'll be discussed. Finally, you'll learn how to configure BlackBerry Maps to always point north, to view your tracking status, clear the map's cache, zoom and pan, and more.

Chapter 12, "Tether Your BlackBerry to Your Computer," shows you how, for a monthly fee, you can tether your BlackBerry to your laptop (or other computer) and access the Internet from the computer through the BlackBerry's cellular connection. You'll need to work through some setup tasks using VZAccess, an application included with your phone, and let Verizon know you plan to tether, and sign up for the required additional service before you can get started, though.

Chapter 13, "Get Music on Your BlackBerry," teaches you how to get music from your computer to your phone using two applications, Media Manager and Media Sync. Both applications are included in the Desktop Manager Software, which you'll need to install on your computer. Once these applications are installed, you can move and sync music you currently manage in Windows Media Player or with iTunes. You can even copy entire playlists and albums, if you like.

Chapter 14, "Search for, Play, and Manage Media Files," guides you through the process of searching for, playing, and ultimately managing the media files on your phone. Here the focus is mainly on music, but photos and videos are briefly discussed. You'll learn to create playlists of your favorite songs too, record personal messages using the Voice Notes Recorder and send them via MMS, and more.

Chapter 15, "Use the Calendar and the Clock," introduces the applications you'll use to create appointments and set alarms and reminders, among other things. You'll explore all of the calendars on your phone (there's one for every e-mail account you've created), and how to create appointments on those specific calendars. You'll also learn how to send an appointment via MMS, create reminders, and configure sounds for those reminders.

Chapter 16, "Explore Applications" introduces a few applications you can perform work with, including MemoPad, Tasks, Word To Go, Sheet To Go, and Slideshow To Go. You can use these applications to perform editing tasks on specific types of documents, like Microsoft Office Word documents, even when you're away from your desk.

Chapter 17, "Verizon Service and Applications" introduces the Verizon-specific applications you can install and use including VZ Navigator for directions, maps, points of interest, local businesses, and traffic, and V CASTMusic for obtaining and managing music on your BlackBerry.

Appendix A, "BlackBerry Tips and Tricks" shows you some unique tips and tricks you may not be aware of, to help you do more, faster! There's a lot of neat information here, so try to commit these tricks and tips to memory.

Appendix B, "Backup, Restore, Reset, and Troubleshoot," offers guidance for backing up and restoring data, scheduling automatic backups, and helpful hints for keeping those backups safe. You'll also learn some tricks for troubleshooting problems online, including visiting BlackBerry's official web site and blog.

PART I

Get Started

1

Getting Started

HOW TO...

- Set up your new BlackBerry Storm2
- Get to know the phone and the Home screen
- Place a call
- Answer a call
- Ask someone to join you in the current call
- Mute a call
- Place a call on hold
- Use the speaker
- Get your voice mail
- Check your voice mail with Visual Voice Mail
- Add a contact manually
- Add a contact from the call log
- Place a call from the Contact list
- Place a voice-activated call
- Pair a Bluetooth device
- Use the new Bluetooth device

Congratulations on your new BlackBerry Storm2! Your BlackBerry smartphone offers more features than ever, including built-in GPS, Wi-Fi support, a camera, and a web browser. It also includes 2GB of onboard memory and a 16GB microSD card. Your BlackBerry enables you to easily keep in touch with others via e-mail or messaging, with pictures and video, and yes, even with a good old-fashioned phone call.

Before you can use the phone, though, you have to insert the battery, charge it, activate it, and set it up. You'll also need to work through the Setup Wizard and brief tutorial that appears when you first turn on the phone. While you can do this on your own, it's probably better if you can do it in a "real" store with a BlackBerry expert, such as a Verizon store where you might have purchased the phone. However, the components only fit together one way, and it's hard to go wrong with the Setup Wizard if you have to do it by yourself.

 The Setup Wizard will ask for your language, time zone, and preferred time format, and walk you through a short tour of the device's features.

Set Up Your New BlackBerry Storm2

After you insert the battery for the first time, the phone should start up and be ready to use. However, the battery likely won't be fully charged, and you should completely charge it before moving forward.

When the phone is charged and ready, click the red icon on the front of the phone. This is technically called the "End" key, and is what brings up the Home screen. Work through the wizard as prompted. Yes is the proper answer in almost all cases. Later, you'll use additional setup wizards to help you configure e-mail, Bluetooth, Wi-Fi, and more. You'll see instructions regarding these wizards in the appropriate chapter in this book.

With that short setup complete, it's time to activate your phone. You should have received instructions for doing this with the BlackBerry from your carrier, likely Verizon. Generally, this consists of:

1. Dialing *228 (or a similar key combination) and pressing 1 to activate and program the phone. Refer to your specific instructions.
2. When prompted to dial 1, or any other number, press the green icon on the front of the phone. This will bring up the keypad.
3. Wait while the phone is activated and programmed.
4. You may receive a message in the message center, notifying you that your phone was successfully activated. You'll know a message is available if a red asterisk appears on the Messages icon. To read the message:
   a. Click the red asterisk on the Messages icon.
   b. Click the message one time.
   c. Read the message.
   d. Click the End key to return to the Home Screen, as shown in Figure 1-1.

 The BlackBerry Storm2 is *supposed to be* exclusive to Verizon. If you purchased an "unlocked" Storm2 from eBay or a third-party seller, though, you may be able to use it with other providers. In this book, we'll only talk about Verizon.

FIGURE 1-1   Click the red asterisk on the Messages icon to read the Verizon
Welcome message and click the red End key to return to the Home screen.

There are some other tasks you may want to perform now:

- On your home or work PC, visit www.verizonwireless.com (assuming you have
  service from Verizon), and register for My Verizon. It's free and allows access to
  the Backup Assistant, entertainment and applications, ring tones, and more.
- Set up automatic billing. If you signed up for My Verizon, click the Overview tab
  and click Set Up AutoPay.
- Back up the data on your old phone to your desktop computer. If your old phone
  is a BlackBerry, use the Backup Assistant at www.verizonwireless/backupassistant
  to transfer your data. If you registered for My Verizon, the service will be free. An
  alternative to the Backup Assistant is BlackBerry Desktop Software, which should
  be included on the software CD that's packaged with the BlackBerry Storm2.
  With it, you can also back up data and synchronization information between your
  phone and PC. If your old phone is not a BlackBerry, take your new phone and
  your old phone to your local Verizon store. They may be able to transfer the data.

Did You Know?

My Verizon

My Verizon is an online account management system that allows you to manage
your account, online, and at any time. You can pay your bill, add or remove
services, view usage (including texts, data, and voice), and set up automatic
payments. You can also browse media like ring tones and wallpaper, among other
things.

- Set up your voice mail. To get started, press and hold the 1 key on the phone. (Press the green Send key to access the Dial Pad.) Setup is self-explanatory and is a short and simple process.

Get to Know the Phone and the Home Screen

Your BlackBerry Storm2 should have come with a pamphlet titled "Explore." That pamphlet will help you better understand the physical aspects of your phone. You'll want to locate the Power/Lock key (located on the top left part of the phone) and the two *convenience* keys on each side. By default, the convenience key on the left side is set to place a call using a voice command; the convenience key on the right is used to open the camera for picture taking. There's a Volume key, too. It's on the right side, toward the top.

 The two convenience keys can be reprogrammed to launch any program by going to Options | Screen/Keyboard.

You'll find keys that act more like buttons (and which I'll sometimes refer to as buttons) on the front of the phone, the part that contains the Home screen. From left to right they are

- **The Send key**   Use this key to place and answer calls, to access the call log, and to view contacts. The Send key is green. See Figure 1-2.
- **The Menu key**   Use this key to view contextual menus that change depending on what application or window is open. When you are using the phone, pressing

FIGURE 1-2   The icons for Send, Menu, Escape, and End are located on the front of your BlackBerry.

the Menu key offers options like Call Voice Mail and View Speed Dial List. The Menu key is the BlackBerry logo, sometimes referred to as the BlackBerry key.

- **The Escape key**   Use this key as you would use the Back key in a web browser or the Escape on the keyboard. Most of the time, it takes you to the previous screen. The Escape key is an arrow shaped like a u-turn symbol.
- **The End key**   Use this key to end a phone call and return to the Home screen. The End key is red.

To help you get acquainted with these features, perform the following tasks:

- Let the phone sit idle for about a minute, and then press the End key. That's the red key on the front of the phone. This brings up the Home screen.
- Let the phone sit idle for another minute until the screen dims, then press the Send key. That's the green key on the front of the phone. This brings up the phone features. To make a call, dial the number and press the Send key again.
- Press the End key and click Messages. Read the introductory message from Verizon. (Press the Escape key to go back to the previous screen.)

 If you want to explore the Home screen, note that the first time you open an application you may be prompted to agree to the terms and conditions and/or download the application. It's OK to do this, but beware, you may be prompted to agree to new monthly fees, such as those associated with VZ Navigator.

Finally, there are three terms you must understand before going any further:

- A "tap" is a light touch, and tapping only highlights choices. You can tap prior to "pressing" a key to make sure you have selected the right option. You won't hear any sounds when you tap the screen.
- A "touch-press," "press," or "click" is a firm press on the screen. You'll hear a click when you've done this correctly. You can use this option to open an item and activate it, like an option on the Home screen or an option on a menu. Throughout this book, this is what you'll do unless otherwise prompted.
- A "scroll" is a scrolling movement you perform with one finger. Scrolling lets you move up, down, left, or right on the screen.

Use the Phone and Control In-Call Sounds

With the phone activated, you can now place and receive calls and work with in-call options. When you press the green Send key, you'll have immediate access to the phone options. You can place calls manually using the Dial Pad, shown in Figure 1-3.

FIGURE 1-3   Notice the three tabs across the top of the screen. To place a call using the Dial Pad, make sure the Dial Pad tab is selected.

 You can make a call manually using the Dial Pad shown here, or you can select a number under the Call Log or Contacts tabs.

Once you're in a call, you can mute the call, use the speaker phone, switch to another call, add a participant, or adjust the volume, depending on the circumstances and the wireless plan and features you selected. You may even opt to ignore an incoming call after viewing the name or number on the screen.

If you miss a call and the person calling leaves a message, you'll need to know how to check your voice mail. You can access your voice mail by doing a long press on the 1 key on the keypad. That's pretty standard; pressing 1 to get to your voice mail has been around for years. As with other features, the first time you use the application you'll need to set it up; just follow the prompts to choose a voice mail option. You'll learn about all this next, and more.

Place a Call on Your BlackBerry Storm2

To place a call, press the green Send button. You can place a call by manually typing a number and pressing Send again.

You can also make a call from the Contacts tab. Under the Contacts tab, just start typing the name of the person to call, and when the name appears, click it. If more than one number is programmed, you'll be prompted regarding which number to call.

You can also place calls from the Call Log. As with the Contacts tab, select the number to call and press the Send button.

FIGURE 1-4   Type the number to dial and press the Send key.

To place a call manually by dialing it:

1. Click the Send button on the Home screen.
2. Type a number using the keypad. See Figure 1-4.
3. Press the Send button again.

 If you type a number that's incorrect, press the back arrow to delete it.

To place a call from the Call Log:

1. Click the Send button on the Home screen.
2. Click the Call Log tab.
3. Click any number in the list. You do not need to press the Send key.

To place a call from your Contact List:

1. Click the Send button on the Home screen.
2. Click the Contacts tab.
3. Type all or part of the contact's name.
4. Click the contact in the resulting list.
5. If necessary, choose from multiple contact numbers.
6. Press the Send key on the phone.
7. To hang up the call, press the red phone button on the Home screen.

Speed Dial

"Speed dial" is a feature allowing you to assign any contact in your contact list to a number on your phone's Dial Pad. Just press and hold a number on the Dial Pad, and when prompted to assign a contact, click Yes. After assigning a contact, to dial that person, you simply press and hold the assigned number key.

If the other party hangs up before you, your call will be disconnected. You will not need to press the red icon to end the call.

Answer a Call on Your BlackBerry Storm2

To answer a call, press the green phone icon on your Home screen. However, it can be a little more complicated than this if you're in a call and someone else phones. Of course, you have to have call waiting as part of your voice plan with your phone service company to accept incoming calls while you're already in one, but most of the time features like call waiting, caller ID, and even call forwarding are enabled by default.

If your phone rings and you can't answer it (or don't want to), quiet the call as soon as you can by pressing the Mute key on the top of the phone. It's on the right corner across from the Power key. It's considered rude to let your phone ring multiple times without answering it while in the presence of others.

To answer a phone call, and then to answer another when you're already in a call (should the need arise):

1. When the phone rings, click the green phone icon to answer it.
2. Press the Volume button on the side of the phone to increase or decrease the volume. You can see the bars that denote how loud the phone currently is on the screen, as shown in Figure 1-5.
3. If you're talking on the phone and another call comes in (someone is "beeping in"), you can either click Answer or Ignore.
4. If you click Answer, the first call will be placed on hold and the second call will be answered. You can then click the Flash key to switch between the two calls.

Ignoring a Call

If you choose to ignore a call, the caller will be sent to your voice mail and will be prompted to leave a message.

FIGURE 1-5   You can see the volume on the screen while in a call, along with other call features like Speaker, Mute, Flash, and Add Participant.

Ask Someone to Join You on a Current Call

While you're in a call, several things appear on the screen, including your phone number (presumably so you can find it quickly if someone requests it), how long you've been connected, the number of the person you're talking to and their name (provided the name is available to you), and options like Speaker, Mute, Flash, and Add Participant. If you are already in a call with one person and another person calls you, you'll use the Add Participant button to add the second caller to the first call.

 There are icons under Flash and Add Participant that let you access things like Show Dial Pad (if you need to "press 1 to speak to a representative"), Notes, Home Screen, Calendar, and View Contacts, if you need to perform other tasks.

To ask someone to join you in the present call, you'll have to first have three-way calling enabled on your BlackBerry's voice plan. If you do, here's how to add another person to the call:

1. While in a call, press the Add Participant button.
2. Place a second call, using the Dial Pad, Call Log, or Contacts list.
3. Once you're in a three-way call, press the Menu button to access additional options, like Flash (detailed later) and Activate Speakerphone.

Muting a Call

The person on the other end of the phone won't know you've muted the phone. If prompted to respond, though, quickly press Mute again to turn the mute feature off.

Mute a Call in Progress

When you are on a call where you have to do most of the listening, like a conference call, you can mute the phone so that you can hear the person talking but they can't hear you. This is a really neat feature when you want to multitask while on the phone, for instance, to feed a baby, answer e-mails at your PC, or even play a video game. You can set the phone on a stand, enable the speaker phone, click Mute, and then go on about your business while still listening to the information being presented.

To use the Mute feature:

1. While in a call, hold the phone so you can view the screen.
2. Press Mute.
3. To disable the mute feature, click Mute again.

Place a Call on Hold

Placing a call on hold is slightly different from muting a call. With Mute, you can hear the conversation but the person on the other end can't hear you (or anything you're doing in the background). With hold, the person on the other end can't hear you, but you can't hear them either. You may want to put someone on hold while you move to a quieter place to talk, or when you need to locate a person, paperwork, or requested information.

To place a call on hold:

1. While in a call, view the screen.
2. Click Flash.
3. Click Flash again to return to the call.

Use the Speakerphone Option to Talk Hands-Free

If you'd like to conduct your conversation hands-free while in a call, you can turn on the Speaker feature. Enabling the speaker sends the call through the BlackBerry's larger speaker instead of through the smaller earpiece. Because it comes though a speaker, it's really loud. There are many reasons to use the Speaker feature when in a call:

- You can't hear the person on the other end due to a hearing problem.
- You can't hear the person on the other end due to the background noise in your immediate area.

- You need to allow others in the vicinity to hear the call, too.
- You need to be hands-free, perhaps to type, to drive, or to write down directions.

 As with Mute, Flash, and Add Participant, you can access the Speaker while in a call from the in-call screen options.

Check Your Voice Mail

Voice mail is a feature that allows callers to leave you a voice message if you can't or don't pick up the call when they phone you. Verizon offers more than one type of voice mail, though, and you can pick the type you want.

All plans come with what's deemed "basic" voice mail. Basic voice mail is the kind you're used to—you press 1 to dial your voice inbox and hear your messages. There's also Visual Voice Mail, which enables you to see your voice mail messages on your BlackBerry screen. You can view, hear, reply to, save, or delete messages instantly, without having to dial in to your voice mailbox. This feature costs extra. There's also Premium Voice Mail. With Premium Voice Mail, you can record up to ten messages and have a specific message play for a specific caller, among other things (and, of course, it costs extra, too). No matter what plan you choose, you have to set it up first to use it.

To set up voice mail, no matter what plan you've selected, you must follow the directions given to you during your phone purchase. At the time this book was written, you could dial *86 from your BlackBerry Storm2 or dial your own wireless number from another touch-tone phone (pressing # during the greeting) to get started. I simply pressed and held the 1 key and was prompted to set up voice mail before I could use it. The setup process is quick, and requires you select a PIN to identify yourself when checking your voice mail.

Once your voice mailbox is set up, you can access your voice mail. To access your voice mailbox and retrieve your messages:

1. Click and hold the 1 key on your BlackBerry's dial pad, as shown in the following illustration.
2. Wait while your voice mail box is accessed.
3. Follow the voice prompts to listen to, delete, and/or save your voice messages.

You can also access the icon for voice mail from the Call Log and Contacts tabs. Figure 1-6 shows the Voice Mail icon at the bottom of the Call Log tab. It looks like a cassette tape.

FIGURE 1-6 The Voice Mail icon is available from the Call Log tab (and the Contacts tab).

Check Your Voice Mail with Visual Voice Mail

There's an option on your Verizon phone plan to add Visual Voice Mail. Visual Voice Mail is a step up from the basic voice mail you're used to. With Visual Voice Mail you can listen to voice mail messages on your phone, without having to dial in to your voice mail inbox. This saves quite a bit of time because you don't have to wait for the phone to dial and connect, and you don't have to listen to the voice prompts once you're connected.

Visual Voice Mail costs a few extra dollars a month (at the time of this writing, $2.99 per month), and you have to install it. Installation consists of a few steps:

- Clicking Visual Voice Mail on the Home screen
- Agreeing to the Terms of Service
- Allowing the program to download
- Agreeing to more fine print and to pay the extra fees associated with the service
- Clicking the Visual Voice Mail icon again
- Typing in your voice mail security code

Once Visual Voice Mail is installed and enabled, click it on the Home screen to "view" missed calls and listen to voice messages:

1. Click the End button or the Escape button to access the Home screen.
2. Turn the phone sideways and locate Visual Voice Mail. (You can also click the wallpaper on the Home screen to view additional icons.) See Figure 1-7.
3. Click the Visual Voice Mail icon.
4. View your missed calls and press the Play icon to hear the message. It will change to a Pause icon during playback.
5. Note the options at the bottom, specifically Callback, Erase, and Reply. (Compose lets you compose voice mails for other Verizon Wireless numbers only.)

FIGURE 1-7   Visual Voice Mail is available from the Home screen and must be installed before you can use it.

Add, Use, and Manage Contacts on Your BlackBerry Storm2

When you maintain an updated contact list, you can easily access contacts from the Contact icon on the Home screen while performing various BlackBerry tasks like text messaging, e-mailing, and dialing. You can choose from a list of contacts and save time by typing just a few letters of the contact's name to access contact information.

You can add a contact by manually typing the contact's name, e-mail address, phone number, and the like, or you can add it with other techniques. One common way to add a contact is to locate it from a call log or e-mail, click the Menu key, and choose Add to Contacts when prompted.

Add a Contact Manually

The most time-consuming way to add a contact is to add it manually. If the contact you want to add has not contacted you on your BlackBerry, and the contact cannot be synced from your desktop PC, this is the route you'll have to take.

Tip Use this method to update contact information and to add additional information like a mailing address, secondary phone number, and more, too.

To add a contact manually:

1. Click the End icon to open the Home screen. (This step will not be included from here on.)
2. On the Home screen, click the Contacts icon, as shown in the following illustration.
3. Press (click) the New Contact button.
4. Type the name of the contact. For now, turn the phone sideways to access the full keyboard, and type entire words while ignoring what's on the screen. You'll learn more about typing later.
5. After you've finishing inputting information, press the Escape key.
6. Click Save.

Add a Contact from the Call Log

All data regarding the calls you place and accept are in the Call Log. You can add people and numbers in this list to your Contacts list easily.

1. Click the green Send key to open the phone options.
2. Click the Call Log tab.
3. Tap a call in the log (tap lightly but do not click) that is not currently a contact.
4. Press the Menu key and select Add to Contacts. See Figure 1-8.

FIGURE 1-8 The Menu key enables you to add any selected contact to your Contacts list.

5. Type the contact information.
6. Press the Escape key.
7. Click Save.

Place a Call from the Contact List

The Contacts list holds information you've added about your contacts in a single scrollable alphabetical list. While the Contact list is open, you can locate and call any contact and edit one easily.

To place a call from the contact list:

1. Click the Contacts icon.
2. Locate the person to call and click or tap their name.
3. Press the Send button.

Tip If your previous phone contains contacts you'd like to have on your BlackBerry, take both phones to your local Verizon store. They can almost always transfer the contacts for you (yes, even from an iPhone).

Place a Voice-Activated Call

Your BlackBerry Storm2 has built-in voice activation. In fact, a convenience key is set up by default so that you can access and use it easily. The convenience key associated with voice activation is the key on the left side of your phone.

It's a good idea to get to know voice activation; you can more easily place calls while driving for instance, even though I'll publicly state that pulling over is always the best option while driving. But hey, if you're going to talk on the phone while you drive anyway, let this feature make it a bit safer for you.

 To place a voice-activated call with a Bluetooth headset, the headset must support this technology.

1. Click the left convenience key. If you've changed the convenience keys and pressing the left key does not open voice activation, press Applications and then Voice Dialing to practice with it now.
2. You'll be prompted to say a command.
3. Say "Call" and a contact name or phone number.
4. You will be prompted regarding what contact or number to call. Say Yes, No, or Cancel to respond.

Set Up a Bluetooth Headset

A Bluetooth headset or other hands-free Bluetooth device, such as a hands-free car kit, lets you talk on your phone through the headset, allowing you to keep your hands off the phone and free for other tasks. Generally, the range of such devices is around ten meters. You won't get a Bluetooth device with your BlackBerry, though; you have to purchase it.

That said, if you've purchased a Bluetooth device, you'll need to charge it (or insert a battery) and then "pair" it with your phone. "Pairing" allows your phone and your Bluetooth device to recognize and communicate with each other. Pairing is what prevents your phone from picking up another person's Bluetooth headset, or trying to connect to other Bluetooth devices like computer keyboards, mice, and so on. Pairing is unique to your phone and your earpiece.

 When purchasing a Bluetooth headset or other device, make sure it's compatible with the BlackBerry Storm2. This will eliminate any problems related to Bluetooth profiles, compatibility, or setup.

Pair the Bluetooth Device

The directions for pairing a device with a BlackBerry differ from one device to another, so specific directions won't be given here. Instead, generic instructions will be included.

To get started with your Bluetooth device:

1. Read and follow any instructions for charging the device.
2. On your BlackBerry, click the Menu key, and click Setup.
3. Click Set Up Bluetooth. See Figure 1-9.

FIGURE 1-9   You have to tell your BlackBerry that you want to enable Bluetooth and locate a device.

4. Click OK to change the name of your device before pairing.
5. Perform any additional instructions for your device, like putting it in "pairing mode."
6. Click Search or Listen to locate the device.
7. After the device has been located, type the passkey or perform any additional steps. The key will be included with your device.

Use the New Bluetooth Device

Using a Bluetooth headset or device requires you to read the instructions that came with the device. There should be directions for:

- Turning on the headset
- Wearing the headset
- Changing the volume
- Making and receiving calls
- Changing headset sounds and tones

2

Explore Messaging

HOW TO...

- Learn about PINs
- Find your BlackBerry Messenger PIN
- Set Up BlackBerry Messenger
- Send a PIN-to-PIN message
- Add another BlackBerry Messenger contact
- Send and respond to BlackBerry Messenger messages
- Change your BlackBerry Messenger availability status
- Move the BlackBerry Messenger icon to the Home Screen
- Send and respond to SMS/MMS messages
- Delete a single SMS or MMS messages
- Delete multiple messages at once
- Learn SMS Shorthand and explore typing tips
- Explore third-party messaging programs

There are other ways to communicate using your cell phone besides actually calling someone and talking to them. You can text a short message, send a picture or map along with a short note, or start a conversation using one of the many instant messaging software options. In this chapter you'll learn about two types of messaging: text messaging and instant messaging, and what each one offers.

Text messaging, as related to the BlackBerry anyway, is the act of typing and then sending short messages from your cell phone to another person's cell phone. The recipient's phone must be capable of receiving text messages, but these days, that's a common feature. It's important to note that you and/or the recipient may incur a small fee ($0.20 or so) for sending and receiving a text message, so before you get started, make sure you understand your own phone service plan and whether you have a flat-fee charge for text messages or a pay-as-you-go plan in place. There are two types of text messages you'll learn to send in this chapter, SMS and MMS.

Instant messaging is quite a bit different from text messaging. Instant messaging requires that you use a program like BlackBerry Messenger, Google Talk, Windows Live Messenger, Yahoo! Messenger, or AOL Instant Messenger (or another) to send messages. These programs are a step up from cell-to-cell text messaging, because they can be sent to and from anyone with Internet access. This means you can hold a conversation with a PC user, for instance, or any other person who has a computer or mobile device with Internet access and a compatible messaging program. It also means that because this type of message is Internet-based, the messages you send and receive are counted as data usage, not text messages, so if you have an unlimited data plan you won't have to pay extra to send and receive these type of messages.

But why send texts or instant messages at all? There are many reasons to incorporate messaging. You might prefer messaging because it provides an easy way to keep any conversation short. Text messages are limited to 160 characters, allowing you to quickly state the purpose of your message and get on with your day. People seem to understand that, too; for the most part, people know that text messages are generally informative, short, and sweet. You may also prefer to send an instant message to a person if you are in a place where you cannot talk on the phone, like a meeting or loud concert, or if you know the person you want to talk with can't currently answer the phone themselves. With instant messages, you can send quite a bit of information.

Communicate with BlackBerry Messenger

BlackBerry Messenger is an instant messaging program you can use to communicate with text messages in real time with other BlackBerry users. BlackBerry Messenger comes preinstalled on the Storm2, but to use the program it must be installed on the contact's BlackBerry, too. You can use BlackBerry Messenger to quickly communicate with other BlackBerry users, and there is no additional cost for sending those messages.

The advantages to using BlackBerry messenger include:

- Carrying on multiple conversations simultaneously with many contacts.
- No-charge messaging to other BlackBerry users.
- Knowing the status of your contacts, including if they're "busy," "available," or "on vacation."
- Personalizing the application with your picture.
- Creating groups of friends, family, or colleagues.
- The ability to send "PIN" messages to contacts. PIN stands for personal identification number, and each BlackBerry has a unique one.
- Access to a complete User Guide from BlackBerry with extensive instructions for performing any task with the application. See Figure 2-1.

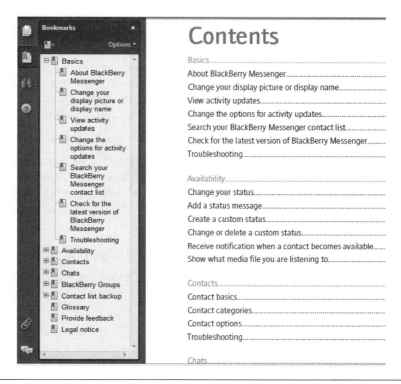

FIGURE 2-1 The BlackBerry User Guide is available online at BlackBerry.com and is quite informative.

There is one specific disadvantage that is extremely limiting when using BlackBerry Messenger:

- Contacts you communicate with must also have a BlackBerry and have installed and have set up the program.

 Most newer phones come with BlackBerry Messenger already installed, like the Pearl, Tour, and Storm1.

Learn About PINs

You may not have caught the significance of the fact that *each BlackBerry device has its own PIN*, but it is quite significant. It means you can send a message to another BlackBerry user by sending the message using the PIN instead of a cell phone number, e-mail address, or contact name.

When you send a message to another BlackBerry user using the PIN, it arrives there quickly—really quickly, like walkie-talkie or pager fast. That's because it doesn't stop along the way at any e-mail servers or network provider servers; it stays within the RIM network. It's more private, too. Your PIN message doesn't get stored in any e-mail inboxes, network mail servers, or sent items folders, or anywhere else for that matter. It's private, much more so than e-mails and texts.

To send and receive PIN messages, you'll need two things. You need your PIN and a contact's PIN.

 A PIN is safe to give out to people you know. It's not a password and it won't allow anyone access to your device at any time. It's kind of like a serial number that defines an appliance or a VIN that defines a car, or if you're a computer geek, a MAC address that defines a PC.

Find Your BlackBerry Messenger PIN

You can share your PIN with others so they can more easily add you to their contacts lists and send you text messages. Locating your PIN is not very intuitive, and thus requires a bit of instruction.

To find your PIN:

1. Press the Menu key, and then click Options.
2. Click Status. See Figure 2-2.
3. Read, share, and/or memorize your PIN.

 To send your PIN in an e-mail, click Messages on the Home screen and compose a new e-mail (see Chapter 7). In the subject line, type **mypin** and click the Space key. Your PIN will appear. (You can ask your BlackBerry-challenged friends to do the same!)

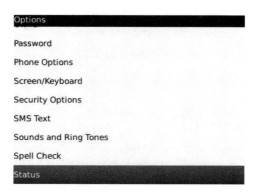

FIGURE 2-2 Click Status to locate your PIN.

Set Up BlackBerry Messenger

Now that you know your PIN and a bit about BlackBerry Messenger, it's time to set it up and get started messaging! There are a few tasks to do, including locating the program, starting it, accepting the terms of service, entering your name as you'd like others to see it, and a few other things. You only have to do this once, though, and there's a wizard that walks you through it. Because you are probably not too adept at entering data, scrolling through terms of service, and performing installation and setup tasks yet, we'll walk through it step by step.

To set up BlackBerry Messenger on your new Storm2:

1. On the BlackBerry menu screen, locate the Instant Messaging icon. Click it.

 Often the term *Home screen* is used to denote the first screen you see with the eight icons on it, while the *BlackBerry menu screen* is the screen you see that contains all the icons. When you're in the Home screen, click the background picture to go to the BlackBerry menu screen.

2. Click the BlackBerry Messenger icon on the next screen.
3. Use your finger to scroll to the bottom of the page and click I Accept.
4. Type your name as you'd like others to see it. Press the Return key on the keyboard when you're finished.

 For now, turn the phone sideways to have access to the full keyboard. You'll learn more about typing throughout this chapter.

5. Click OK when prompted that you'll have to add a contact to communicate with others.
6. Click the Add a Contacts button (if you know a BlackBerry user).
7. Type the name of a contact you know, their BlackBerry PIN, or an e-mail address. They will be sent a message and will appear as "pending" until they accept your offer. See Figure 2-3.

 Remember, you need to add a contact that owns a BlackBerry device!

Did You Know? **Add Yourself as a Contact!**

If you don't have any BlackBerry contacts, for practice you can add yourself! When you send a message to yourself later, you'll be able to see it send and watch it be received on your phone.

FIGURE 2-3   You have to add a contact in order to communicate with BlackBerry Messenger.

Send a PIN-to-PIN Message

Sending a PIN message is a good place to start with messaging, and will help you learn how to navigate the Messages screen and type in the message window. It will also help you to connect with your contacts more quickly than if you used other methods. If you don't have anyone's PIN yet, that's OK, though. Just skip to the next section and come back here when you do.

To send a PIN-to-PIN message:

1. From the Home screen, click the Messages icon.
2. Click the Compose button. (Alternatively, you can press the Menu key and then select Compose PIN.)
3. Click PIN, as shown in the following illustration.

4. Type the PIN in the To: field. This won't be an easy task if it's the first time you've done it. However, here are some tips:
   a. Turn the phone sideways to view the full-screen keyboard.
   b. Use the keys on the keyboard to switch the layout to type numbers or capital letters. You'll have to experiment here to get a feel for the keyboard.
   c. If a word appears that matches what you're trying to type, click the Space key to accept it, or press it with your finger. This probably won't happen with a PIN, but you can apply it in another message.
   d. Press the Enter or Return key on the keyboard to move to the next line.
5. Type any subject or message.
6. Click the Send icon in the top-right corner of the screen.

You can see your sent message in the Messages list, as well as any responses to your message.

It's much easier to send a PIN-to-PIN message to someone if their PIN is in their contact information on your BlackBerry. To add a PIN for an existing contact, select the contact from your Contacts list, click the Menu key, and click Edit.

Add Another BlackBerry Messenger Contact

PIN-to-PIN messages are nice, but not everyone knows or shares their PIN. Generally, BlackBerry users are more likely to become a contact—and opt for BlackBerry Messaging texts. Before you can send an instant message to someone, though, you have to request permission from that person to exchange messages with them. You'll learn to do that next. This keeps people from sending unsolicited messages (such as Spam) to your BlackBerry (or your contact's).

To add a BlackBerry Messenger contact from your address book and to obtain permission to send the messages:

1. Open BlackBerry Messenger.
2. Click Add a Contact.
3. Type the first letter of the contact you'd like to add and scroll through any list that appears to locate the contact you want. Click it.
4. Click Send, as shown in the following illustration.

To add a BlackBerry Messenger contact for a person not already in your address book:

1. Open BlackBerry Messenger.
2. Click Add a Contact.
3. Click in the top window and type a PIN or e-mail address.
4. Click Send.

The contact will have to receive and then accept your invitation. Once that happens, the contact's name will appear in your contact list. If you can, before continuing, add a few more contacts.

Invitations that you receive from others will appear as messages. You'll need to accept or decline invitations if you receive them.

Send and Respond to BlackBerry Messenger Messages

Now the fun can begin! With a contact or two you can start sending and receiving messages. Keep in mind that messages are meant to be short and the recipient should be able to respond with only a few words; if you need to write something longer, consider sending an e-mail.

To send a text and respond to one you've received:

1. On the Home screen, press the Messages icon.

Don't see what you think you're supposed to? Click the Escape key. You may be viewing a message you started to compose earlier.

2. Click Compose.
3. Click Instant Message and then select BlackBerry Messenger.
4. Click a name in the contacts or conversations list. See Figure 2-4.
5. Type your message.
6. Press the Return key on the keyboard to send the message.

Did You Know?

Using Shortcuts

Many people use shorter versions of words and phrases to lessen what they have to type. LOL means "laughing out loud." BBL means "be back later." BTW means "by the way," and NRN means "no reply necessary." For more information, search the web for "IM shorthand" or refer to Table 2-1 later in this chapter.

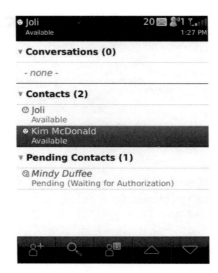

FIGURE 2-4   Choose a contact from the list to create a message.

Change Your BlackBerry Messenger Availability Status

Your availability status shows your contacts whether you are available for exchanging instant messages or you are busy. You can be Free to Chat, Busy in a Meeting, On Vacation, Out of Office, Available, and Unavailable. If you haven't responded quickly enough to a message you've recently received, BlackBerry Messenger will automatically change your status to Busy. It may also be changed to Busy if the BlackBerry knows you're doing something else on your BlackBerry. Your status will change to Unreachable if you're talking on the phone or in an area without enough wireless coverage to support messaging.

   To change your status:

1. Open BlackBerry Messenger.
2. On the Home screen of BlackBerry Messenger (not in a conversation window), click the Menu key.

Did You Know?

Caps Key

When you click the Caps key and then type a capital letter, the default keyboard reappears. If you need to type multiple capital letters, hold down the Caps key for a second first. Then, the all caps keyboard will remain on the screen until you repeat the process to bring up another keyboard.

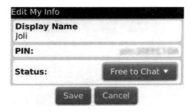

FIGURE 2-5 Change your status to something like Free to Chat or Unavailable.

3. Click Edit My Info.
4. Use the options next to Status to change your status to something else. Here, I've selected Free to Chat. See Figure 2-5.

 If you set your status to Unavailable, you won't be notified when instant messages arrive.

Move the BlackBerry Messenger Icon to the Home Screen

If you decide you like BlackBerry Messenger and plan to use it often, consider moving the icon for it to the Home screen. You can move any icon to the Home screen in this manner, or to another folder or area on your BlackBerry.

To move the BlackBerry Messenger icon to the Home screen for easier access:

1. On the BlackBerry menu screen, click Instant Messaging.
2. Tap, but do not click, BlackBerry Messenger.
3. Press the Menu key.
4. Click Move to Folder.
5. Click Home. See Figure 2-6.

FIGURE 2-6 Move the application icon to the Home screen.

Communicate with SMS and MMS Messaging

You learned in the introduction that messages such as SMS and MMS are cell-to-cell communications. You also learned you have to pay for each message sent and received. You may have a plan that allows you to pay as you go, you may have a plan that allows a specific number of texts for a set fee, or you may have unlimited messaging. You'll need to find out before you start texting, as shown in Figure 2-7. Ready?

SMS stands for Short Messaging Service; MMS stands for Multimedia Messaging Service. SMS is text messaging; MMS is "picture" messaging. SMS messages contain text. MMS messages can contain text plus pictures, animation, sound, and even video. Both options are considered a form of instant messaging, and most cell phones and cell phone plans support this popular texting technology.

Unlike proprietary messaging programs like BlackBerry Messenger, with SMS there's nothing to download, and the service is not limited to specific phone manufacturers, third parties, or users. To send an SMS or MMS message, you only need to know the cell phone number of the person you want to send the message to. You don't have to know their PIN or e-mail address, or request them to install the instant messaging program you're using, or even add you as a contact or buddy. You don't even have to send an invitation or get their permission. It's pretty easy.

Send, Reply, and Forward SMS and MMS Messages

Billions and billions of text messages are sent every year by BlackBerry users, iPhone users, Palm users, and from popular prepaid phones like the AT&T GoPhone, as well as almost every other kind of cell phone. Because SMS is a service, SMS messages can be sent to any kind of phone that supports it. This means you can send a text message from your BlackBerry to a contact with an iPhone without problem.

To send an SMS text message:

1. On the Home screen, click the Messages icon.
2. Click the Compose button and choose SMS Text.

FIGURE 2-7   You can view your text and "pix" usage online at Verizon Wireless.

SMS and MMS or Messages?

You can press the SMS And MMS icon on the Home screen instead of the Messages icon. The steps are basically the same.

3. If the contact is not in your address book:
   a. Type an SMS phone number.
   b. Click OK.
   c. Type the message and press the Enter key on the keyboard to send it.
4. If the contact is in your address book:
   a. Type the first few letters of the contact's name, as shown in Figure 2-8.
   b. Select the contact from the results and click OK. (If the contact has multiple contact numbers, select the proper one.)
   c. Type your message.
   d. Press the Enter key on the keyboard.

To send an MMS message:

1. On the Home screen, click the Messages icon.
2. Click MMS.
3. If the person is in your address book, scroll through the list or type the first few letters of their name to locate them.
4. Click the name and if additional contact options are given, select one.
5. If the contact is not in the list, click the Menu key, and click Add a Contact. Add the contact information before continuing.

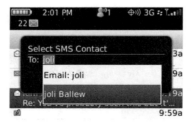

FIGURE 2-8   It's easier if you can select a contact you already have.

6. Type the message and press the Enter key. If you want to attach something before sending:
   a. Press the Menu key.
   b. Select the type of attachment to include (Contact, Appointment, Picture, Audio, Video, Voice Note).
   c. Navigate to the file and select it.
   d. Click the Mail icon to send.

 To reply to an SMS or MMS message, simply click the message and type your reply.

Manage MMS and SMS Messages

Messages can easily add up and can become hard to manage. This will become clearer to you the more messages you send and receive. As the list gets longer, you'll start to look for ways to manage the messages. Your first step is to delete ones you no longer want.

You've probably seen the Delete option under a list of messages. And sure, you could diligently click Delete, choose how to delete the message (which may offer On Mailbox & Handheld, On Mailbox, or Cancel depending on the message type), and repeat as needed. But that is tiresome, especially if you have a lot of messages to delete. There are better ways.

You can also save certain messages, flag them for follow-up, search through messages you have, and more. What options exist depend on the type of messages you're viewing. Since we're only talking about text and instant messages in this chapter, though, we'll leave our focus on those.

To delete a single SMS or MMS message:

1. Click SMS And MMS on the Home screen to view these kinds of messages.
2. To delete a single message, tap it, and click the Delete key on the bottom of the screen. The Delete key is the key with the red x on it.
3. Click Delete.

 If you get tired of Step 3, which is confirming that you really do want to delete a message after pressing the Delete key, you can change this behavior. Tap a message, press the Menu key, and click Options. Under General Options, change Confirm Delete from Yes to No.

To delete multiple messages at once:

1. In any message list, tap the first message to delete. Leave your finger on that message.
2. Tap another message further down the message list with another finger. All messages in between will be selected.
3. Click Delete. The Delete option is shown in Figure 2-9.

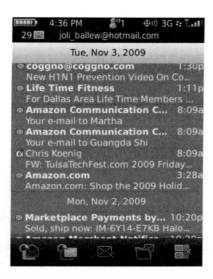

FIGURE 2-9   You can select multiple messages to delete using two fingers to select the first and last message in a list. Scroll toward the top or bottom of the list to select all messages.

For the most part, at least to start, deleting unwanted messages will do in keeping your message list organized and manageable. There are other ways to manage messages, though, and there's just not enough room in this book to go over all of the options. However, here are a few tips to get you started:

- To see a list of messages by a single person (and to hide the rest of the messages), tap and hold the contact name.
- To move to the top or bottom of a message list, click and hold the Scroll Up or Scroll Down buttons on the shortcut bar at the bottom of any message window.
- When reading your messages, you can quickly slide your finger to the left or right to see the previous or next message in the list.
- When pressing on a single person's name, you may also see a threaded text chat view where you can see the whole text history in chronological order and you don't need to slide your finger left or right to see the previous or next message.

Learn SMS Shorthand and Explore Typing Tips

You've had a little experience typing in this chapter, and if you've followed my advice, you've turned the phone sideways to type entire words using a full keyboard. That's one way to type, but many people swear by "SureType." SureType works by guessing what you're going to type based on the keys you press, and it learns the more you type. You can see how this works by typing a word like *awesome*.

FIGURE 2-10   Typing with SureType takes a little getting used to.

When you look at the SureType keyboard, you'll see that the letters are grouped together a certain way. If you press the A key followed by the W key to type the word "awesome," you don't get an A and a w. You get what's shown in Figure 2-10.

You have several choices when this happens. You can:

- Scroll through the list of suggestions and tap Aq, which will get you nowhere.
- Ignore the suggestions and keep on typing and press the Space key when you've typed the entire word (which helps the BlackBerry "learn" and is recommended for a while at least).
- Type until you see the word you want and select it from the menu of suggestions (or press the Space key to accept a highlighted word), which will shorten the keystrokes you have to input.

You can also use Multitap. Multitap looks like SureType but for each letter you want, you select it from the list. For instance, to type *awesome*, you'd click the AS key, and click A from the suggestions, click the QW key and select AW from the suggestions, click the AS key again and click AWS from the selection, and so on. I can't imagine why this option would be better than SureType or using a full keyboard, but to each his own, right?

You can create AutoText entries to make typing easier. You'll learn about that in Chapter 4.

SureType keeps words it knows in the dictionary. You can add words there that it doesn't already know, like your company's name, a product name, a foreign word, a child's name, and more. To access the dictionary, click Options, and then Custom Dictionary. Press the Menu key, click New, and add your own entries. Press the Enter/Return key when finished.

And finally, Table 2-1 offers some common shortcuts you'll see in text and instant messages people send you, and messages you can use yourself.

TABLE 2-1   Messaging and Typing Shortcuts

Shorthand	What It Means
4E	Forever
ASAP	As soon as possible
B4	Before
BBL/BBS	Be back later/Be back soon
BTW	By the way
FWIW	For what it's worth
IOU	I owe you
OIC	Oh, I see
RUOK	Are you OK?
W8	Wait
:-)	I'm smiling right now
:-D	I'm laughing right now
;-)	I'm winking at you
:-(	I'm not happy about that
(((H)))	Hugs
:-O	Yawning (bored) or surprised or shocked, depending on the person's interpretation of the shortcut

Use Third-Party Messaging Services and Applications

In order to fully understand what third-party messaging offers and whether you can benefit from it, you'll need to briefly review the programs and services introduced in this chapter. So far, we've looked at BlackBerry Messenger and SMS/MMS services.

To recap, BlackBerry Messenger is an instant messaging program that allows BlackBerry users to communicate, at no additional cost, with other BlackBerry users via text and group chat. BlackBerry Messenger is an application that must be installed on the BlackBerry, and the program can only be used to communicate with other BlackBerry owners. The upside to this program is that when you text another BlackBerry user, you aren't charged any texting fees. The downside is that you can only communicate with other BlackBerry users who have agreed to exchange texts with you and who also have the BlackBerry Messenger software installed. If you like this kind of messaging, but you want to communicate with non-BlackBerry users, you'll need to choose a third-party instant messaging program.

SMS and MMS are services (not programs) included with most voice plans that allow you to text anyone with an SMS- or MMS-enabled cell phone and data plan. Some voice plans include unlimited texts; others charge per text, generally 10 to 25 cents. You can't hold group conversations as you can with instant messaging programs, but you can communicate via text to virtually any cell phone user. Practically every phone offers SMS and MMS messaging.

If you prefer using an instant messaging program, versus simply sending and receiving texts via SMS and MMS, perhaps because you'd like to hold group chats, know the status of your contacts, create your own status, apply specific ring tones to contacts, or to access an existing contact list, you'll want to choose a third-party instant messaging program. If you like the idea of BlackBerry Messenger but need to connect with contacts that use an iPhone, for instance, a third-party instant messaging program is the option you're looking for.

There are lots of third-party instant messaging programs you can install on your BlackBerry, and there's no way to cover them all here. There are a few you've likely used on your computer, and you may already have a contact list or an affinity for one or the other. There are four options already built in:

- Windows Live Messenger
- Yahoo! Messenger
- Google Talk
- AOL Instant Messenger

If you have an ID for any of these and would like to use it, click the icon for the program you want to use. You'll be prompted to download the program and agree to the terms of service.

Once installation is complete (and it may look as though you have to download and install it again, but you don't), click the Escape key to get back to the Instant Messaging window. Agree to any terms of service, and log in with your existing ID. See Figure 2-11.

FIGURE 2-11   Log in with your existing ID.

If the screen goes dark during installation, click the Escape key to return to the last window you had up.

Once you're logged in, you'll have access to your contacts and be able to instant message with them as usual.

3

Use Your Camera

HOW TO...

- Remove and insert the memory card
- Format the memory card
- Save data to the memory card
- Delete data on the memory card
- Encrypt data on the media card
- Take a picture and share it in various ways
- Use zoom and flash
- Configure camera options
- Browse for and show a picture
- Create a slideshow of pictures
- Access pictures from the Media folder
- Record video
- Play back recorded video
- E-mail a video

Your BlackBerry Storm2 has a 3.2-megapixel digital camera that allows you to take pictures and video and share them with others. The Storm2 also comes with a 16GB microSD card for storing the images you acquire. It comes with a flash, built-in image stabilization, and a digital zoom you can apply by dragging your finger up or down the screen.

In this chapter, you'll learn how to use your camera and your memory card. You'll learn how to insert and configure the card should you ever need to remove or replace it, and you'll learn a little about securing that card should it ever get stolen. Following that, you'll learn how to take pictures and video, and use all of the available picture and video tools (like zoom, flash, and various configuration options for quality and size).

Use the Memory Card

The Storm2 comes with 2GB of onboard memory and a 16GB memory card. It's difficult to say exactly how many pictures, songs, videos, and applications you could store with this amount of memory, but it should be enough for a long time. While not an exact science, it's generally agreed that, for a BlackBerry Storm at least, 1GB of memory can hold about 1,500 high-quality pictures **or** 250 songs, and you'll likely have a combination of these. Remember, though, you won't just be taking and saving pictures and downloading music—you'll also have video, applications, ring tones, and other data. Video takes up the most space (much, much more than pictures or music), so if you plan to take a lot of video, make sure you manage that video by deleting data you don't want to keep or moving it off the card onto a computer regularly.

 You can encrypt the data on your memory card and make it nearly impossible for someone to steal your card and access the data on it using another device.

There are several makes and models of media cards, and your BlackBerry Storm2 accepts the smaller card type, the microSD card. These cards, made by various manufacturers, come in several sizes and are capable of storing any kind of data you like.

Remove and Insert the Memory Card

Your SD memory card should have come preinstalled in the phone. It should have been inserted into the appropriate slot under the back cover and you should never have to worry about it. If it was not preinstalled, there are instructions in this chapter, and instructions should have also come with the phone.

Before you start, though, note that there's really no reason to remove the card unless it gets full and you do not want to move the data on it to a computer. When you connect your phone to a computer, the computer will see the phone *and the card*, and you can access the information on the card just as if you'd physically removed the card and inserted it into a card reader. You can then copy or manage the data as desired. Figure 3-1 shows data on a BlackBerry's media card, as shown from a Windows Explorer window.

There are a few other reasons you would want to remove the card—if it becomes damaged or unreadable or if you want to give the card to someone else to share the data on it.

To remove or insert the media card:

1. Turn off your phone and remove the back cover.
2. To be extra safe, remove the battery.
3. Look for the memory card. It should say SanDisk on it.
4. Slide the media card down and out of the slot to remove it, or slide it in and up to insert it.
5. Replace the battery, replace the back cover, and turn on the phone.

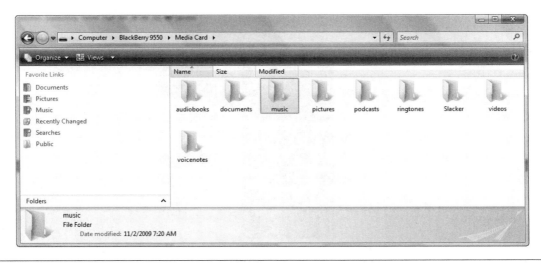

FIGURE 3-1   When you connect your BlackBerry to your computer, the computer can read the data on the memory card just as if you'd inserted the card into a memory card reader.

    To view the amount of memory available on the card, click Options on the BlackBerry menu screen and click Memory. The last item on the screen shows the available device memory space.

Format the Memory Card

By default, music, pictures, applications, videos, and similar data are stored on your memory card. Formatting the card erases everything on it. You will rarely need to format the card. However, if you come across a reason to wipe clean the memory card installed in your BlackBerry, here's how.

To format the media card:

1. On the BlackBerry menu screen, click Options. (If you're on the Home screen, click the background picture to get to the BlackBerry menu screen.)
2. Click Memory.
3. Click the Menu key again.
4. Click Format. See Figure 3-2.
5. When you're prompted to format the media card or device memory, choose media card.
6. Click Yes to complete the formatting process.

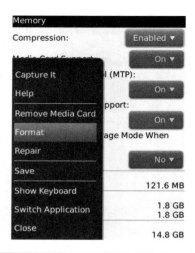

FIGURE 3-2   Click Format only if you're sure you want to erase everything on the
card.

Save Data to the Memory Card

To save data to the memory card, you'll need to have memory card support enabled.
You can check to see if this is configured correctly from the Media Card Support field
in Media Card option. The next time you save data, like a picture, music, or video, it
will automatically save to the card instead of the onboard memory. It's highly likely
that the settings are already correct, but just to be sure, you can check.

To turn on (or off) media card support:

1. On the BlackBerry menu screen, click Options.
2. Click Memory.
3. Verify Media Card Support is set to On. If it is not, click Off and select On.
4. Click the Escape key.
5. Click Save.

 The first time you take a picture, you may be prompted to save the picture to the
memory card. Choose Yes to enable memory card support.

Delete Data on the Memory Card

You can delete all of the data on a memory card by formatting it, as described earlier.
However, it is not likely that you'll want to delete all of the data on the card at any
time. Most of the time you'll only want to delete specific data like pictures, videos, or
songs. To delete only specific data requires that you select the data and delete each
piece manually. For instance, to delete pictures, you'd go the Pictures folder, select the
pictures to delete, and opt to delete them. The same holds true of videos and music.

FIGURE 3-3   Select a single piece of data to delete and press the Delete key to delete it.

To delete data stored on your media card:

1. From the Home Screen, click Media.
2. Choose Music, Videos, Pictures, Voice Notes, or other category that contains data you want to delete.
3. To delete a single item, tap the item to select it and press the Delete button (the big red X) on the bottom of the screen. Click Delete when prompted to complete the task. See Figure 3-3.
4. To delete an entire folder of data, tap the folder name and click Delete. Click Yes when prompted to complete the task.

If you need to delete data that is not a single piece of data or an entire folder, connect your phone to the computer. You can manage media more efficiently from there. You'll learn more about data management in Chapter 13.

Encrypt Data on the Media Card

It's pretty easy to remove a media card from a BlackBerry phone. If someone were to take your media card, they could probably access the data on it simply by inserting the card into a generic media card reader using any PC. You can protect that data by encrypting it.

FIGURE 3-4   Once you enable encryption, additional options appear.

 You can also protect others from accessing data on your phone by requiring a device password and by locking the phone when you aren't using it. If someone were to steal the phone, they'd have to input the password to use the phone or obtain access to the data stored in internal memory. There's a Lock icon on the BlackBerry screen and an Unlock button on the top of the phone. You'll learn more about this in Chapter 4.

To encrypt data on the media card:

1. From the BlackBerry menu screen, click Options.
2. Click Security Options.
3. Click Encryption.
4. Change Encryption from Disabled to Enabled.
5. Configure the settings as desired. By default, encryption of media files is disabled. If desired, change No to Yes for both options. See Figure 3-4.
6. Click the Escape key and, when prompted, click Save.

 If you're prompted to create a device password, do so. For more information on passwords, refer to Chapter 4.

Use the Camera

The first step in using the camera is to locate the Camera convenience key or the BlackBerry menu screen icon. Clicking either opens the camera application. Before taking a picture, you can focus or zoom, or set the quality or size easily via the Menu button's Options. Once you've taken a picture, you can then view it on the phone, send it via e-mail or MMS, or set the picture as a contact picture or wallpaper. You can also rename the picture easily. You can even post your pictures to web sites like Facebook or MySpace.

Take a Picture and Share It in Various Ways

There are a couple of ways to take a picture. You can press the Camera icon on the Home screen or press the convenience key on the outside of the phone. By default, the camera is assigned to the bottom key on the right side. If you haven't changed the convenience keys, using the external key is the easiest. Press the key once to access the camera, press it halfway to focus on your subject, and press it again to take the photo. You can also take a picture using the camera's on-screen icons.

After you take a picture, icons appear on the screen to allow you to e-mail the picture, set the picture as a contact picture or wallpaper, take another picture, rename the picture, or delete the picture. If you take the time to perform the desired task immediately after snapping a photo, you'll be well on your way to managing your media efficiently. At the very least, delete pictures immediately if you know you don't like the shot and don't want to keep the picture.

To take a picture and immediately share the picture via e-mail, set it as a contact picture, delete it, or perform other tasks:

1. Click the convenience key on the bottom-right side of the phone. If you've changed the settings, locate Camera on the Home screen.
2. Press the button halfway to focus in on your subject.
3. Press the button all the way down to take the picture.

 If the convenience key does not control the camera because it's been changed from the default settings, tap the Camera icon on the screen to focus in on your subject and click the icon to take the picture.

4. To delete the picture, click the red x.
5. To rename the picture, click the Folder icon and type a new name for the photo.
6. To send the picture via e-mail (or BlackBerry Messenger, Facebook, or MMS), click the Mail icon. (See Chapters 7 and 8 for more information on sending an e-mail.)
7. To set the picture as your Home screen background or to assign it to a caller as their caller ID picture, click the Set Picture As icon. Choose Caller ID or Wallpaper. If you choose Caller ID, select a contact from the contact list that appears.
8. To take another picture, click the Camera icon.

Use Zoom and Flash

You can zoom in on your subject and then zoom out if desired prior to taking a picture. Zooming in can help you get a better shot by making the subject appear larger and closer in the photo. If, after zooming in, you decide you don't want to zoom, you can zoom back out. (If you need to zoom out but can't, simply take a few steps backward!) You can zoom in or out using the convenience keys on the right side of your BlackBerry, the ones that normally control the volume, or you can use your finger to scroll up to zoom in and scroll down to zoom out.

FIGURE 3-5   Easy access to camera options makes configuring settings for a single shot an option, every time.

The flash is set to *automatic* by default and will flash when the camera believes it's warranted. You can quickly turn off or on the flash by clicking the Menu key and selecting Options. The Camera Options page, shown in Figure 3-5, offers access to all of the settings you'll need prior to taking a picture, including the option to turn on or off the flash.

To take a picture and use the zoom feature and flash:

1. Open the camera application by pressing the convenience key on the bottom-right side of the phone or the Camera icon on the Home screen.
2. Tap the Camera icon on the screen or half-press the Camera convenience key to focus in on the subject.
3. Use either method mentioned earlier to zoom in and out of the subject.
4. Point the camera toward a dark area (perhaps to the ground) and notice the flash appears briefly.
5. To turn on or off the flash instead of accepting its automatic setting, click the Menu key, and click Options.
6. Choose the default flash setting to use for this shot and all future ones.
7. Click the Escape key and click Save to apply the setting.
8. Click the Camera icon or the convenience key to take the picture.

Configure Camera Options

You know how easy it is to access the camera options. While the camera application is open, simply click the Menu key and click Options. While that part is easy, knowing what to change and when is a bit more trying. Here is a bit of information about each option, and why you may want to change it from its default.

- **Default Flash Setting**   Automatic is a good option to use most of the time. The camera knows how much light is available, when a flash is required, and when one is not. However, in some instances turning the flash on or off is a better option. You may want to turn the flash off if a mirror is part of the shot or constantly produces redeye in a subject, or turn the flash on to make a scene appear brighter than it is. (You can also use the camera and flash as a sort of flashlight, should you ever need to locate your keys in the bottom of your purse!)
- **Autofocus**   Normal is a good option in most cases. However, there are two others: Close Up and Off. Select Close Up if you're, well, close to your subject. Select Off if Normal is unable to focus the shot effectively.
- **Image Stabilization**   By default, image stabilization is turned off. If your pictures are blurry because of slight movements you make when taking the picture, consider turning image stabilization on. You can also turn on this feature when taking pictures in low light without a flash to help improve the stability of the image.
- **White Balance**   The setting is Automatic. Without going into detail about what white balance is and getting into a long discussion about filters and such, let the other White Balance options speak for themselves: Sunny, Cloudy, Night, Incandescent, and Fluorescent. If your picture just doesn't look right and it's cloudy outside, try Cloudy.
- **Picture Size**   The picture size describes and defines how large or small the picture actually is in terms of pixels. Pixels are the tiny dots that make up the photo. Large is 2048 × 1536 pixels, Medium is 1024 × 768 pixels, and Small is 640 × 480 pixels. The more pixels, the better quality the image, but the more space the image takes up on your memory card, and the longer it'll take to e-mail. If you know you're going to e-mail the image after taking it or apply it to a contact, consider small or medium. If you plan to print the shot, use it as wallpaper, or for any other reason want a higher-quality shot, choose Large.
- **Picture Quality**   Size and quality go hand in hand. There are three options: Normal, Fine, and Superfine. Superfine is the highest quality and also takes the most space on your memory card. As with Picture Size, consider a lower-quality image for pictures you know are for e-mail, contacts, or Facebook, and Superfine for images you plan to print.
- **Color Effect**   There are a few color effects you can apply to a shot: Black and White, Sepia, and Whiteboard. Experiment with effects to see what each applies. Consider applying the Black and White effect to create a photo that looks "old," for instance.
- **Geotagging**   When this setting is enabled, information regarding your location will be included in your media files, in the form of latitude and longitude data. If you ever forget where a particular picture was taken, you can use that information to find the location on a map.

- **Store Pictures**   Store Pictures should be set to Media Card, not Internal Memory. You media card has 16GB of space while internal memory only offers 2GB.
- **Folder**   This option allows you to change the default folder where your pictures are stored. Generally, the defaults are fine. However, you can click the Folder icon and select an existing folder or even create a new one. Click the Menu button to create a new folder and then select it.

View and Show Pictures

It's easy to view and show pictures you've just taken using your BlackBerry; while you're in the Camera application, click the Menu button and click View Pictures. The Pictures folder will open and offer access to any folders you've created and the shots in them. Once you're in the Photos folder, you can click the furthest-left icon to toggle between View Icons and View List.

 You can also access pictures from the Home screen. Click Media, and click Pictures.

To view and show a single picture while in the Camera application:

1. Take a picture.
2. Click the Menu button.
3. Click View Pictures.
4. Scroll through the pictures list or thumbnails (icons) and locate the picture to view. Click it to view it full screen.
5. Use your finger to scroll left and right to move through the pictures in the selected folder.

To show a slideshow of pictures:

1. With the camera application open, click the Menu button and click View Pictures.
2. Tap any folder that contains pictures to view as a slideshow, or tap a single picture in this list.
3. Click the Menu button again and click View Slide Show. See Figure 3-6.

 Press the Escape key to stop the slideshow.

Access Pictures from the Media Folder

If you've already closed out the camera application, or you simply want to show and view pictures you've already taken, you can access your pictures in the Media folder. There, you can do all of the things with pictures you can do from within the Camera application, including delete, e-mail, set as a contact picture, and more.

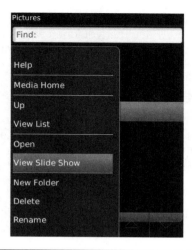

FIGURE 3-6 You can easily offer a slideshow of your favorite pictures from your pictures folders.

To view pictures stored in your Media folders:

1. From the Home screen, click Media.
2. In the Media folder, click Pictures.
3. Browse the images as detailed earlier. Tap an image to select it. Click the Menu key to access the following commands:
   - **Set As** To set the pictures as a "Caller ID" (that's a contact picture) or as wallpaper.
   - **View List (or View Icons)** To change the view of the folder from a list to thumbnails or vice versa.
   - **Open** To open the picture in full screen mode.
   - **View Slide Show** To show the pictures in the folder as a slideshow.
   - **Properties** To view the image properties including the name, size, date created, date modified, and other data.
4. With a photo selected, you can also click the e-mail icon to send the photo via e-mail, MMS, Facebook, or BlackBerry Messenger, or click the red x to delete it.

 If you've paired your phone with another Bluetooth device, you can send a photo using Bluetooth.

Take Video

Recording video is a lot like taking pictures, except that you have to tell your BlackBerry you want to capture video first (instead of simply taking a picture). Once you're in video camera mode, you simply press the record button one time to start recording, and once more to stop. Recorded video takes up quite a bit of space, though, so make sure that you immediately delete video that you don't want to keep and occasionally move video off your BlackBerry and onto a computer to keep your media card from getting full.

Record Video

As noted earlier, to take a video you need to enable the video camera and press the Record button. That will do most of the time, but sometimes you'll want to configure special settings—like color effect or lighting. Just as there are settings for picture taking, there are settings for video recording. There aren't nearly as many as there are for pictures, though; in fact, there are really only four you need take an interest in:

- **Video Light** This is the video camera's version of the "flash." When Video Light is turned on, a light will also shine while you're recording video. This can greatly reduce battery life, though, and should only be used when absolutely necessary.
- **Color Effect** There are two color effects: Black and White and Sepia. Unless you want to apply these effects to video you record, leave the setting to Normal.
- **Video Format** Normal (480 × 352) is the default, but if you plan to send video via e-mail or MMS, opt for MMS Mode (320 × 240).
- **Store Videos** Make sure you store your videos on your memory card, not internal memory.

So, before you start to record, click the Menu button and Options to review these settings. Once you're sure they're the way you want them:

1. Start the camera. Remember, you can start the camera from the bottom-right convenience key or by pressing the Camera icon on the Home screen.
2. Click the Menu button and click Video Camera. (Alternatively, you can select the Media app from the BlackBerry menu, and then click on Video Camera.)
3. To configure options, click the Menu button again and click Options. Make any changes desired, click the Escape key, and click Save.
4. When you're ready to record, click the Record button. Take your video and press the Record button again to pause the recording.
5. While paused, you'll have options at the bottom of the screen: Continue Recording, Stop, and Play. Underneath are Send, Rename, and Delete. For now, either click Stop or Continue Recording.

Play Back Recorded Video

Some of the time you'll share video you record by playing it back on your phone. You can do that the same way you view and share the pictures you take. You can either click the Menu button and then click View Videos while in the camera application, or open the Media folder and click Videos.

To play back recorded video on your phone from the video camera application:

1. If you've just recorded video on your camera, you'll have access to the Play button. To view this button, record some video now. Click the Play button to view the video.
2. If you've recorded video and the phone has dimmed, the Play button will not be visible. To view the video:
   a. Click the Menu key.
   b. Click View Videos.
   c. Click the video in the list to view it. See Figure 3-7.

E-mail a Video

It is possible to e-mail a video provided the video isn't very long. For best results, try to keep any video you want to e-mail to 2 minutes or less. Once you've recorded video, it's easy to e-mail it:

1. Locate the video in the Videos folder. (On the Home Screen, click Media, and click Videos.)
2. Tap the video to e-mail.
3. Click the Menu key.
4. Click Send As E-mail.

 E-mailing is detailed in Chapters 7 and 8.

FIGURE 3-7   A list of videos is available from the Videos folder. Click any video to play it.

How Do Videos Play?

By default, videos that you e-mail to PC users will play using a program called QuickTime.

You can send a short video in an MMS message, too. Before taking the video, though, make sure to record the video with MMS Mode, detailed earlier. Proceed as above, but this time, select Send As MMS in Step 4.

If you've paired your phone with another Bluetooth device, you can send a short video using Bluetooth.

PART II

Personalize Your BlackBerry

4

Change Your BlackBerry's Look and Feel

HOW TO...

- Add your name and a welcome message
- Apply a password
- Change your Home screen background (wallpaper)
- Change the ring tone
- Change the volume and settings for a ring tone
- Apply a ring tone to a contact
- Reposition the Home screen icons
- Hide a Home screen icon
- Unhide a hidden icon
- Move an icon
- Change what the convenience keys do
- View and change AutoText entries
- Add your own AutoText entry
- Use an AutoText shortcut
- Choose the right accessories

There are a lot of ways to personalize your BlackBerry. You can choose ring tones, customize the background, reposition the icons, change what the convenience keys do when you press them, and even add accessories like wireless speakers or hands-free headsets. Personalizing your BlackBerry can make it more fun to use, but it can make it easier to use too. For instance, if you're constantly looking up information on BlackBerry Maps, you can assign that application to a convenience key on the outside of the phone. You can assign any application you like, or leave the keys set to their defaults.

Configure Owner Information and a Password

Your owner information appears on the BlackBerry screen when the phone is locked. You can type in your name and address as a safety measure. If you lose the phone or if the phone is stolen, and if the police or an upstanding member of society finds it, you'll have an increased chance of getting your phone back.

In addition to adding your personal information, you should also consider applying a password. A password will keep thieves, kids, or coworkers from accessing any personal information stored on your BlackBerry if you ever leave it unattended or if it ever falls into the wrong hands.

 Engrave your name on the phone for even more security.

Finally, you can further personalize the phone by applying a Home screen picture. Your BlackBerry comes with several to choose from, or you can choose a picture you've taken, copied, or downloaded.

 Consider a picture of yourself for the Home screen picture. This picture may help you recover the phone if it's ever lost or stolen.

Add Your Name, Phone Number, and Perhaps a Welcome Message

The owner information contains your name and various information you choose to include. You might want the welcome message to include your home phone number with a plea to call you there if the phone is ever lost or stolen. Because the information appears on the Home screen when the phone is locked, if you want, you can even type yourself a welcome message!

To add owner information:

1. On the BlackBerry menu screen, click Options.
2. Click Owner.
3. Type your name and other information.
4. Press the Menu key.
5. Click Save.

Apply a Password

To lock your device, you simply click Lock on the BlackBerry menu screen. However, with no password applied, unlocking the phone only involves pressing the (un)lock button on the top of the phone (on the left side). If you configure a password to protect the data on your BlackBerry, though, when the device is locked, the password must be input before it can be unlocked. If the person who finds your phone can't unlock it, they can't use it to make calls, view your e-mail, or surf the web.

You may recall that data is stored on the memory card inside the phone, and unless that card is encrypted, anyone can remove the card and view what's on it using another device, like a computer.

To apply a password:

1. On the BlackBerry menu screen, click Options, as shown in the following illustration.

2. Click Password.
3. Set the Password field to Enabled. See Figure 4-1.
4. Click Set Password, type the password, and type it again to confirm it. You'll have to press the Enter key after inputting the password.

 Your password will need to meet certain requirements for length, and cannot be a sequence, among other things. Don't worry about that, though; just type the password you want and see if it passes the password test!

5. Configure any other options as desired.
6. Press the Menu key.
7. Click Save.

 If you decide later you don't want to use the password, disable it in the Password field. (You'll have to input your password to do this.)

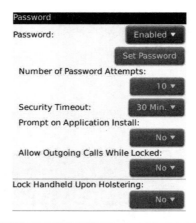

FIGURE 4-1 Set the Password field to Enabled, and then configure additional settings.

 You can change the password under Security Options, Password.

Change Your Home Screen Wallpaper

The background picture, called *wallpaper*, is what is shown on your Home screen when the phone is locked, and what you see behind the half-screen Home screen when the phone is in use. You can change the picture to just about anything at all.

While a picture of your dog, children, boat, or favorite landscape is nice as a background picture and really personalizes your phone, consider a picture of yourself. If you use your own picture, lock the phone when it's not in use and add your name, contact information, and a message that says something like, "I've misplaced my phone, this is my picture. Do you see me anywhere near?" you just may get your phone back.

To configure a new Home screen background:

1. On the BlackBerry menu screen, click Media.
2. Click Pictures.
3. Locate the picture you'd like to set as your new Home screen background. Click it to open the picture in a full window.
4. Press the Menu key.
5. Click Set As.
6. Click Wallpaper. See Figure 4-2.
7. Click the End button two times to see your new background.

 Have someone take a picture of you, and then click the Menu icon and Set As to apply it as your Home screen background.

FIGURE 4-2   Set the picture as "wallpaper."

Apply Ring Tones

A *ring tone* is what you hear when someone calls you and the phone rings. You can choose from several built-in ring tones or you can download your ring tone of choice from the Internet. Once a ring tone is applied, you can change the volume and settings for the ring tone, including having the phone vibrate while it rings. In addition, you can set a ring tone for a specific contact in your contact list; if you wanted, you could configure a different ring tone for every contact you have. Configure a specific ring tone for a specific contact and you can tell who's calling without even looking at the phone. (I have an old-fashioned telephone ring assigned to my 89-year-old dad, for instance.)

Change the Ring Tone

A ring tone is what distinguishes your phone from other phones in the vicinity. It's important that your ring tone is different from the tones of the person that you spend the most time with—otherwise, when you hear a ring you won't know if it's your phone or theirs! To change the ring tone for all calls, simply select the ring tone from the list of available ring tones. Later, you'll learn how to change a ring tone for a specific contact, and even later, how to download new ring tones from the Internet.

To change your ring tone for all calls:

1. On the BlackBerry menu screen, click Sounds.
2. To quickly change the ring tone from say, Loud to Vibrate Only, click the desired setting:
   - **Normal**   The basis for other options. Normal is not too loud, not too soft, and has preconfigured tones for e-mail, instant messages, reminders, and other settings.
   - **Loud**   A louder ring tone than Normal, with similar alerts.
   - **Medium**   Another ring tone option with preconfigured settings for ring tone, message alerts, and reminders.
   - **Vibrate Only**   A setting where the phone only vibrates when a call is received, with "silent" configured for other alerts, like e-mail messages.
   - **Silent**   With this setting, the phone makes no noise at all, and will not even vibrate when a call arrives.
   - **Phone Calls Only**   Choose this setting to only hear sounds when a phone call arrives.
   - **All Alerts Off**   With this setting, all alerts are disabled.
3. To configure a ring tone, click Set Ring Tones/Alerts.
4. Click Phone.
5. Click the arrow next to Ring Tone. A list will appear. See Figure 4-3.
6. Click Try It to hear the tone.
7. Continue to configure settings as desired, for instance, to use vibration with the ring tone, show the LED when a call arrives, or set the volume.
8. Press the Menu key.
9. Click Save.

FIGURE 4-3   Change the ring tone from Set Ring Tones/Alerts.

Did You Know?

What Does Active Mean?

The active ring tone will have the word "Active" by it. If Normal is the current setting, the option for Normal will read Normal (Active).

Change the Volume and Settings for a Ring Tone

When you're entering a meeting, movie theater, or library, you'll want to change your ring tone to Silent, Vibrate Only, or All Alerts Off, to minimize disruptions to others in the building or room. You do that by clicking the Sounds icon on the BlackBerry menu screen and selecting the appropriate option. In some instances, though, you'll only want to change the ring tone volume. If you're entering a noisy club, subway, or party, you will want to increase the volume of the ring tone. If you're having dinner at home, watching TV, or visiting a friend for a quiet evening in, you'll want to decrease the volume of the ring tone.

It's easy to change the volume for any ring tone, and some ring tones have settings, too. To change the volume and settings for a ring tone:

1. Click Sounds.
2. To change the ring tone volume for the *active* sound profile, click Set Ring Tones/Alerts.
3. To change a custom sound profile, click Custom Profiles. Click a profile.
4. Click Phone.
5. Click the arrow next to Volume to select the appropriate volume. See Figure 4-4.
6. Press the Menu key.
7. Click Save.

FIGURE 4-4 The volume for an active ring tone can be changed using a scale of 1 to 10, 10 being the loudest.

Apply a Ring Tone to a Contact

You can apply a specific ring tone to a contact so that you can tell who's calling without looking at the phone. You may want to assign an alarm ring tone for an elderly parent, the song "Who let the dogs out?" for your pet's vet or groomer, or a favorite TV theme song for your children. Go wild! You simply can't imagine how helpful it is to be able to tell who's calling without having to pull the phone out of your purse or pocket and look at the caller ID until you've experienced it firsthand. Once you get used to it, you'll wonder how you ever did without *auditory* caller ID.

   To apply a ring tone to a contact:

1. On the Home screen, click Contacts. (If you don't see a list of contacts, click the Escape key.)
2. Tap the contact to which you want to apply a ring tone.
3. Press the Menu key and click Edit.
4. Scroll down to Custom Ring Tones/Alerts and click Phone.
5. Choose the ring tone to apply in the Ring Tone field.
6. Click the Menu key, and click Save.

Reposition the Icons, Hide and Move Icons, and Reconfigure the Convenience Keys

You can personalize your BlackBerry in many ways. You already know you can change the background picture and ring tones, but did you know you can reposition the icons? If you change the order of the icons and hide the icons you don't use, you can make your BlackBerry much easier to use. There's no point in wasting time scrolling through unwanted icons on a cluttered Home screen. Remove them!

   You can also change what the convenience keys do when you press them. If you recall, the convenience keys are the buttons on the left and right side of your phone, and they are configured with specific functions, like starting the Camera application. If you use a specific application regularly, like Calendar or Media, assign it to a convenience key.

Reposition the Icons

You can reposition icons on the Home screen to change which icons appear where. You may want to put your eight favorite icons in the top eight positions. This will enable you to see and access those eight icons from the Home screen without having to click to get to the BlackBerry menu screen. You can access those eight positions without pressing the End key, which means you can access your favorite applications more quickly.

FIGURE 4-5   Select an icon to reposition, click the Menu key, and click Move to get started.

To reposition an application icon:

1. Click the background picture on the Home screen to view all of the available icons.
2. Highlight (select) the application icon you'd like to reposition on the screen. (Tap the icon one time.)
3. Click the Menu key.
4. Click Move. See Figure 4-5.
5. The icon now has a square around it.
6. Tap gently where you'd like the icon to be moved to.
7. Click the Menu key, and click Complete Move.

Hide or Move Icons

There are a lot of icons on the Home screen. There are eight on the Home screen, and when you click the background picture, you'll see many more on the BlackBerry menu screen. You can hide applications you don't use, or those that don't work, to manage what is shown. Here's an example: VZ Navigator is a nice application and tells

Did You Know?

Reposition Application Folder Icons, Too

You can apply these same steps to icons inside application folders. This means you can reposition icons in say, the Media folder or the Instant Messaging folder, and cause them to appear in any order you'd like.

you all about traffic and routes and getting where you want to go faster, but it costs about $10 a month to subscribe. If you don't want to subscribe, it isn't going to work, and there's no reason to leave the icon on Home screen.

You should know there are a few icons you can't hide, like Options and Manage Connections. Although you can't *hide* those icons, you can *move* them to a different folder. For instance, you may want to move the Manage Connections icon to the Setup folder. If you need it, you can find it in Setup, and when you don't need it, it won't be in your way. And speaking of moving icons, there may be icons you don't want to hide, but just want to get off your Home screen. You can do that as well.

 If you do move icons around, try to move them someplace intuitive. Manage Connections seems to fit well in Setup, for example.

To hide an icon:

1. On the BlackBerry menu screen, select (tap) an icon to hide.
2. If Hide is an option, click it. See Figure 4-6.

To unhide an icon:

1. On the BlackBerry menu screen, click the Menu key and click Show All.
2. Select the icon to show (it will be grayed out), click the Menu key again, and click Hide.
3. The icon will now be available to use, but other hidden icons will still appear grayed out on the screen. Click the Menu key again.
4. Show All will have a check by it. Click Show All to "rehide" the rest of the hidden icons.

FIGURE 4-6   If you don't play games, you can hide the Games icon.

If Hide is not an option, you'll have to move the icon to get it off the Home screen:

1. Select the icon to move by tapping it once.
2. Click Move.
3. Click the new location.

Change What the Convenience Keys Do

Your phone has convenience keys on the side of it. These keys let you access your favorite applications and features quickly. You don't have to settle for what your BlackBerry thinks is the best use of these keys, though; you can change what they do. You may want to apply a certain application to a key to further personalize your phone and to make it easier to use.

To configure a convenience key to open the application of your choice:

1. On the BlackBerry menu screen, click the Options icon.
2. Click Screen/Keyboard.
3. Change the Right Side Convenience Key Opens or Left Side Convenience Key Opens fields, as shown in Figure 4-7.
4. Press the Menu key.
5. Click Save.

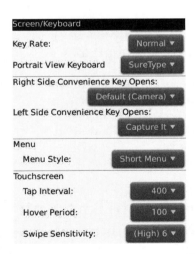

FIGURE 4-7   You can change the convenience keys to open what you want, including third-party applications.

Create Your Own AutoText Entries

AutoText is a feature that allows you to enter shortcuts for words you type often. When you type the AutoText entry for a word, the entire word is spelled out in your message, and you don't have to type it. For instance, you might create an AutoText entry for your entire business name, and have it automatically insert when you type "biz" followed by the Space bar.

AutoText entries exist (and can be created) for commonly misspelled or mistyped words, too. For instance, if you type **hte** and press the Space bar (which is the move you make to accept the AutoText entry that pops up on your screen), your BlackBerry will replace it with *the*, its AutoText entry. This AutoText entry is already available.

To understand how AutoText works, it's best to start by looking at the entries already in your BlackBerry, add a few of your own, and then put AutoText to work in a real-life application.

 Think about the shortcuts you already use, like LOL. See if there's already an entry for it, and if not, create one. For LOL, you might add I'm laughing out loud!, or something similar.

View and Change AutoText Entries

Before you start adding your own AutoText entries, check to see what's already there. You may find what you're looking for, but you may also find existing entries you want to use or change. If you can commit some of these entries to memory and/or change them to meet your needs, you can type quite a bit faster by applying them where possible.

To view and change AutoText entries:

1. On the BlackBerry menu screen, click the Options icon.
2. Click AutoText. Review the entries.
3. Click any AutoText entry to change it.
4. Change the AutoText entry if desired.
5. Press the Menu key.
6. Click Save.

Add Your Own AutoText Entry

Add your own AutoText entries to personalize your BlackBerry and to make typing easier. Think about what you type often, and how you could shorten it with a personalized entry. I have an AutoText entry, JB, which automatically inserts my name, Joli Ballew, each time I type it and press the Space bar.

1. On the BlackBerry menu screen, click the Options icon.
2. Click AutoText.

3. Press the Menu key.
4. Click New.
5. In the Replace field, type the text to replace.
6. In the With field, type the text you'd like to apply.
7. Press the Menu key.
8. Click Save.

Use an AutoText Shortcut

Using an AutoText shortcut is easy. Just type it, and when the pop up appears above it on the screen, press the Space bar to accept it.

To use an AutoText entry:

1. Open any application that allows you to type.
2. Type any shortcut for an existing AutoText entry.
3. Press the Space bar to apply the AutoText entry.

 Opt for Specified Case when you want to create an entry like UCLA (for ucla or Ucla), that should always be capitalized. Opt for Smart Case when you want your BlackBerry to decide on the case based on how you've typed it (asap = as soon as possible; ASAP = AS SOON AS POSSIBLE).

Add Accessories

You can outfit your BlackBerry with various accessories. The most common accessories are cases and "skins" for protecting the phone, hands-free devices, and those related to automobiles, like dashboard mounts and cradles. However, there are plenty of other accessories available. To see just how many accessories there are, visit www.Amazon.com and search for *BlackBerry Accessories*.

Before you purchase any accessory, make sure it's compatible with your BlackBerry Storm2. There are a few accessories you "should" have, like a protective case, screen protectors, and car chargers, but there are others you may simply want, like wireless speakers or hands-free headsets. You may also want to explore:

- Keyboards
- Extra chargers and batteries
- Speakers

5

Download Ring Tones, Wallpaper, and Themes

HOW TO...

- Create a bookmark for http://mobile.blackberry.com
- Locate and download a ring tone
- Apply the ring tone
- Locate and download a wallpaper
- Apply the wallpaper
- Locate, download, and install a theme
- Get started with applications and games

There are a lot of ways to simply have fun with your BlackBerry. You can download ring tones to make your phone sound different from other phones; assign wallpaper to give your phone a different look; or select a theme to apply related icons, sounds, and wallpaper that can really make your phone stand out above all others. You can also download and play games, and select and download applications that are useful to you (like those that let you update your Facebook page or listen to Internet radio). And best of all, you can obtain, apply, and use all of this right at your BlackBerry; you don't even need a computer!

In this chapter, you'll learn how to obtain ring tones, wallpapers, and themes via BlackBerry's Mobile web site. Ring tones and wallpapers are free, but you'll probably have to pay for themes. To do this, you'll navigate to the desired web site using your web browser, select the item you want, and download and install it. This isn't the only way to get these types of applications, though; you can use BlackBerry App World, already on your phone. App World will be detailed in Chapter 6.

Create a Bookmark for http://mobile.blackberry.com

There are several ways to download and install applications and data, including downloading directly from the BlackBerry Mobile web site, using BlackBerry App World, and downloading the data to a PC and syncing the phone with it. In this chapter, we'll focus on the former; here you'll learn how to use your BlackBerry to search for, locate, download, and then install a ring tone and wallpaper from BlackBerry's web site using the browser on the phone. You'll also learn how to download a theme from a third-party site via BlackBerry Mobile, if no free themes are available. If you'd rather use the App World application on your phone to obtain ring tones and applications, skip to the next chapter.

Since you're going to have to navigate to the Mobile BlackBerry web site to download data using the method outlined in this chapter, you may as well create a bookmark for it so you can more easily access it later. If you've never navigated to a web site before, you'll need some specific instructions for doing so. Here they are; if you already know how to navigate to a web site and save a bookmark, you can skip this section.

To navigate to the official BlackBerry mobile web site and create a bookmark for it:

1. From the BlackBerry menu screen, and click Browser.
2. Click the back arrow one time to delete the *www.* part of the address already inserted in the address line, as shown in Figure 5-1. (If you don't see this, click the Menu button and click Go To.)
3. Type mobile.blackberry.com. Hold the phone upright to type the URL using the smaller keyboard, or turn it sideways to access the full keyboard.
4. Press Go.
5. Click the Menu key and click Add Bookmark.
6. Click in the Name line and when the keyboard appears, use it to type a descriptive name for the site.
7. Click the Enter key when finished.

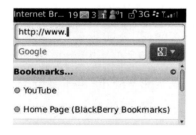

FIGURE 5-1 You want to type mobile.blackberry.com, and you don't need the www.

To access the bookmark later, click the Menu key, click Bookmarks, and scroll through the bookmarks to locate it. Click once to go to the web site.

Locate and Download a Ring Tone from Mobile.BlackBerry.com

Now that you know how to navigate to BlackBerry's Mobile web site, you can browse and download ring tones. The nice thing about the BlackBerry Mobile site is that there are lots of free ring tones. This isn't the case with many third-party sites; many require you to pay for the "good" ring tones.

1. If you need to navigate to the site using your bookmark, click the Menu button, click Bookmarks, and then scroll through the resulting list to go to the page.
2. Scroll through the page to locate Personalize Ring Tones. Turn the phone sideways and click the Zoom In button one or two times if it's hard to see.

 You can double-tap the screen to zoom in as an alternative to using the Zoom button.

3. Click Ringtones, shown in Figure 5-2.
4. If this is the first time you've used the web site, you'll have to agree to the terms of service.
5. You can now access a list of free ring tones.
6. When prompted:
   a. Click Open to hear the ring tone. Click the Back button after it's played.
   b. Click Save to save the ring tone to your phone. Note where the ring tone will be saved. It should save to Media, Ring Tones, My Ring Tones. Press the Enter key on the keyboard to continue. When you see the download has completed, click the Escape button on the phone to return to the previous screen.
   c. Click Cancel to select a different tone.

 Make sure you have an unlimited data plan before downloading too much data from the Internet. Otherwise, you may find yourself with a hefty cell phone bill!

FIGURE 5-2   Locate the option to download ring tones.

Where Are Ring Tones Stored?

By default, ring tones you download are saved to Media under Ring Tones, in a subfolder named My Ring Tones.

Apply the Ring Tone

Once you have downloaded a ring tone, you'll need to apply it. You can apply it to all calls or to a single contact, or to multiple contacts. You make changes in the Sounds application, using the same method you used in Chapter 4 to personalize the phone with ring tones, change the ring tone volume, and change other phone-related sounds.

To apply your new ring tone:

1. From the Home screen, click Sounds.
2. Click Set Ring Tones/Alerts. (You will have to click the Escape key to get here if you don't see this option on the screen, but instead see a configuration window.)
3. Click Phone.
4. In the Ring Tone field, click Browse. See Figure 5-3.
5. Scroll down to the bottom of the list to locate the new ring tone. Click it.
6. Press the Menu key.
7. Click Save.

FIGURE 5-3   When you want to apply a ring tone you've downloaded, you have to "browse" for it.

Download Wallpaper and Themes

Wallpapers and themes can help you change the look of your BlackBerry. Wallpapers change the Home screen picture. You can download wallpaper from the Internet or use a picture of your own.

A theme, on the other hand, changes many aspects, including but not limited to the wallpaper, ring tone, and even Home screen icons. Themes can even apply changes to your convenience keys and sounds. As with ring tones, you can obtain free wallpapers from BlackBerry's Mobile web site. At the time this book was written, though, there were no free themes, only a link to the bplay.com site, where themes can be purchased.

Locate and Download Wallpaper

The wallpaper you choose affects the Home screen image. You can use any wallpaper already on your BlackBerry, you can use a picture you've taken or acquired, or you can download and opt for something you find on the Internet. One place to find wallpaper is the official BlackBerry Mobile web site. You can visit this web site from your phone at: http://mobile.blackberry.com. Once you're there, simply browse the wallpaper to locate the one you want.

To locate and download wallpaper from the official BlackBerry mobile web site:

1. If you need to navigate to the BlackBerry Mobile web site, use the bookmark you created in the first section of this chapter:
   a. Click the Menu button and click Bookmarks.
   b. Scroll through the resulting list to go to the page.
2. Scroll through the page to locate Personalize Wallpapers. Turn the phone sideways and click the Zoom In button one or two times if it's hard to see.
3. Click Wallpapers. If prompted, accept the terms of service.
4. Scroll through the available wallpapers and click Download when you see one you like.
5. The wallpaper will appear on your screen in the web page window. Click the Menu key and click Save Image to save it to your phone. See Figure 5-4.
6. Press Enter on the keyboard, noting the picture name.

Did You Know?   **Save and Apply Any Picture as Wallpaper**

You can download and save almost any picture you find on the Internet and use it as wallpaper.

Apply the Wallpaper

Once you've chosen a wallpaper and downloaded it, you can apply it from the Media icon. The steps you apply to a downloaded wallpaper are the same steps you'll take to apply any image to the Home screen.

1. On the BlackBerry menu screen, click the Media icon.
2. Click Pictures.
3. Click All Pictures.
4. Highlight the wallpaper you just downloaded.
5. Press the Menu key. Press Set As.
6. Click Set As Wallpaper.

Locate, Download, and Apply a Theme

You can apply a theme to your BlackBerry that will change more than just the wallpaper. A theme can also change the look and size of the icons, the quality and sound of the ring tone, and even allow you to customize the icons that appear. To obtain themes from your phone, you can visit this web site: http://mobile.blackberry.com. Themes are great additions and there are thousands to choose from. In this example, I'll choose a theme that completely changes the look and feel of the phone; you'll be quite surprised!

 At the time this book was written, the BlackBerry Mobile site did not offer any free themes, only a link to bplay.com, where themes can be purchased. There are lots of places to get themes, though, including Crackberry.com and through BlackBerry App World.

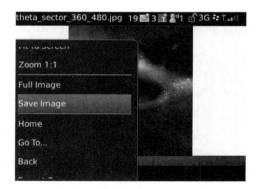

FIGURE 5-4 You'll need to tell your BlackBerry you want to save the picture after you've viewed it.

To locate, download, and apply a theme via the BlackBerry Mobile web site:

1. If you need to navigate to the BlackBerry Mobile web site, use the bookmark you created in the first section of this chapter:
   a. Click the Menu button and click Bookmarks.
   b. Scroll through the resulting list to go to the page.
2. Scroll through the page to locate Personalize Themes. Turn the phone sideways and click the Zoom In button one or two times if it's hard to see.
3. Click Themes. If prompted, accept the terms of service.
4. If you see any free themes, browse through them and work through the download process as detailed earlier for wallpaper. If you don't see any themes, you'll have to visit a third-party web site like bplay or Crackberry.
5. If you decide you like a theme, from bplay or another third-party web site, you'll probably have to buy it. See Figure 5-5.
6. Work through the purchasing process, if applicable. This can be a rather lengthy process on your BlackBerry due to the art of typing in the information on such a small screen, and you may find it better to purchase software via App World instead, detailed in Chapter 6.
7. Once the payment process has completed, click Download and/or Download Now.
8. You may be prompted to enable the theme after the download has completed. Click Yes if desired. You can now apply the theme:
   a. Click Options.
   b. Click Theme.
   c. Select the theme to apply.
9. As shown here, themes apply device-wide changes to your phone. In Figure 5-6, the BlackBerry looks more like an iPhone than a Storm2!

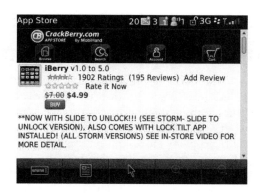

FIGURE 5-5 If you opt for a theme on Crackberry.com or another third-party web site, note that you may have to purchase it.

FIGURE 5-6   Themes can change just about everything about your BlackBerry.

It's possible to select a theme that will make it hard to follow along in this book. If you've found a theme you like, consider keeping it disabled until you've finished learning all you need to learn from this book.

Get Started with Applications and Games

You can download and install applications, games, productivity tools, maps and navigation tools, and more from the Internet. However, you can't get these things directly from http://mobile.blackberry.com in the same manner you obtained ring tones and wallpapers. Obtaining applications is more akin to obtaining themes in the last section, using third-party sites, and paying with a credit card or PayPal.

Instead of going that route, though, and obtaining your applications from a third-party web site, consider BlackBerry App World first. App World is already available on your phone; you just have to set it up. Once you've done that, you can browse, pay for, download, and install just about any application imaginable, and it's often easier than working through a third-party web site. Just look at all of the categories of applications available from App World!

Hey! My Screen Went Black!

It's OK if your screen goes dark during the download process. The download will continue. Just press the Menu key to return to the screen.

You may not want to install or use App World. You may not find what you want there if you do. For the sake of completeness, then, here's how to obtain an application from a third-party web site, specifically CrackBerry.com:

1. From the Home screen, click Browser.
2. Click the Menu button and click Go To.
3. Click the Back button one time to remove the *www* from the address, and then type **m.crackberry.com**. Hold the phone upright (not sideways) to type the URL using the smaller keyboard. Just type the key once that contains the letter to add, and your BlackBerry will figure out where you want to go.
4. Use the Zoom In button to see the web page, if necessary.
5. Click Free BlackBerry Apps directory or Free BlackBerry Storm Apps Directory. Scroll through the free applications.
6. Click any application to start the download process. Click Download when it becomes available. (You may be asked to grant the application trusted status; if so, click Yes if you trust the application.)
7. When the permission page appears, if you trust the application, click Yes to give it the desired status. Press the Escape button to begin the download process.

 You may have to choose your device and model before you can download an application from a third-party site like Crackberry.

8. To locate your new application, on the BlackBerry menu screen, click Downloads, shown in Figure 5-7.
9. Click the application in the Downloads folder to complete setup and/or use the application.

 Remember, you can move applications to the Home screen or to another folder as detailed in Chapter 4.

FIGURE 5-7   Downloads are stored in the Downloads folder.

6

Use BlackBerry App World

HOW TO...

- Install BlackBerry App World
- Get a PayPal Account
- Explore the My World screen
- Search applications by category and download and install a free application
- Choose a featured item, pay for it with PayPal, download it, and install it
- Move an app to the Home screen
- Review an app
- Contact a vendor
- Remove an app

BlackBerry App World is a storefront you can access from your phone. With App World, you can purchase games, social networking applications, news and weather applications, and productivity applications, to name a few.

The first time you access App World, you'll notice that you have the option to view what's available by category, what's free and what costs money, or you can search keywords. There's even a place to read reviews of applications before you get them, or review them after you've used them. You can search for and download just about any application you can imagine, from those that assist with online shopping to a game like Tetris to an app that helps you find the best airfares.

To use App World, you'll need a PayPal account. It's easiest to set up that account on a PC, and once you've set up the account, you only need to enter the information into App World to get started. After you've found and downloaded an application you want, your new app will appear on your BlackBerry, where you'll install, configure, and use it.

Install BlackBerry App World

You can't use App World until the application is installed on your phone. There's a link to get started in the Application Center. If you've never installed an application, this will be a good introduction on how to do it, and after you've done it once, you'll find that future downloads and installations will come quite naturally.

To install BlackBerry App World:

1. On the Home screen, click Application Center.
2. Click BlackBerry App World. If it's already been installed, it'll say Installed underneath, as is shown in Figure 6-1. If it says Not Installed, continue with the remaining directions here.
3. Click Install.
4. Scroll to the bottom of the page and click Download.
5. Choose your language and click Next.
6. Click Download again. Wait while the download process completes.

 If the screen goes dark, press the Menu key to return to the screen to watch the download process.

7. Reboot when prompted, by clicking Reboot.
8. If you're prompted by the Welcome center, click Close after reboot. You can now click App World on the Home screen to get started!

FIGURE 6-1 BlackBerry App World may already be installed, as shown here. However, if it says Not Installed, click to install it.

Get a PayPal Account

PayPal is a way to send money via the Internet. You have to set up a PayPal account to purchase applications from BlackBerry App World. PayPal is the only way to pay for the applications you buy, and thus is required.

PayPal allows you to set up payment options so that funds are taken from your bank account or debit card, or are charged to a credit card you own. PayPal allows you to purchase items online without having to input credit card or bank account information each time, which creates more convenient and secure transactions. Thousands of online merchants accept PayPal, including Wal-Mart, Sears, Barnes and Noble, and eBay.

To obtain a PayPal account using a PC:

1. Visit www.paypal.com.
2. Click Sign Up.
3. Select your country and region. You'll also want to choose the type of account to select.
4. Type your e-mail address first. Choose your primary e-mail address, the e-mail address you use for most of the e-mail you send and receive.
5. Type a password that's at least eight characters. Remember, you'll be typing this password when you want to purchase something online using your BlackBerry.
6. Type your first and last name, your address, and other required information, and click Create Account.
7. Input payment information to designate the bank account or credit card you want to use.
8. Continue inputting additional information as required. Your account will be created when you're finished.

Explore BlackBerry App World

The BlackBerry App World icon is available on the BlackBerry menu screen. Click it to see a featured item with arrows that allow you to move through a graphical list of other featured items, along with icons across the bottom. The icons from left to right are

 After pressing any button (Categories, Top Free, Top Paid, Search, or My World), click the Escape button to return to the previous screen.

- **Categories**   Click here to view apps in categories ranging from Business to Weather.
- **Top Free**   Click here to view free apps listed in order of their popularity.
- **Top Paid**   Click here to view apps you have to pay for, listed in order of their popularity. See Figure 6-2.
- **Search**   Click here to type the name of a specific app.
- **My World**   Click here to view your current downloads and other information.

FIGURE 6-2 Icons across the bottom of the application window let you browse available applications by their type, or category.

Look for the following on the My World screen after you've downloaded and installed a few applications (note that you may not see anything yet!):

1. Any apps you've purchased through PayPal.
2. Any items you've downloaded that are free or trial software.
3. The current status of the item. Some possible states include:
   - **Installed**   The item is currently installed.
   - **Uninstalled**   The item has been uninstalled.
   - **Unavailable**   The item is not currently available. This can happen when you switch phones but continue to use the same App World account. Some items may not be compatible.
4. The progress of items currently being downloaded.
5. Available upgrades for paid or free items.

Locate and Download a BlackBerry App

To get an application from App World to your phone requires you to find, download, and if required, pay for the application. You can browse available applications in various ways; by what's currently featured, by what's downloaded the most, or by the type of application it is. Once you've downloaded your new application, you can access it from the My World screen.

Browse by Category and Download and Install a Free Application

App World applications are categorized by type. When you visit the App World and click the Categories button, you'll see categories for Business, Entertainment, Finance, Games, Health and Wellness, IM and Social Networking, Maps and Navigation, Music and Audio, and many more. Click any category to see the applications in it. Once you choose an application, you can read reviews, view screenshots, and more, right from the phone. This can help you decide if the application is worth the price (or perhaps the bother).

To browse applications by category and download and install a free application from App World:

1. Click the App World icon on the BlackBerry menu screen.
2. Click the Category button.
3. If necessary, drill down into the subcategories.
4. If you find a free application you like, click it to start the installation process.
5. Click Download, Reviews, Recommend, or Screen shots as desired.
6. Click Download when you're ready. The app should install automatically. If you're prompted that installation is complete, click OK or opt to run the application now, if applicable.

 Some applications will ask for Application Permissions. If you downloaded the application and installed it, and you trust it, it's fine to give the application the permissions it requires.

7. Press the Escape key in App World to return to the App World screen that allows you to access the My World button. You may have to press this button more than once. Click the My World button to view the installed program.
8. Press the new app in the My World screen to run it (there will be more on this later).

Choose a Featured Item, Pay for It with PayPal, Download, and Install it

You won't always be so lucky to find free applications. Some of the applications you'll want will require that you pay for them. If you've already set up a PayPal account, and you should have, once you have found an application you want to purchase, simply click Purchase and follow the prompts.

In the last section, you located an application using Categories. This time, I'll show you how to browse featured apps. Note that you don't have to choose a featured app; you can try the Search option, browse Top Paid, or browse Top Free. What you're doing here, though, is working through the process of paying for an app prior to downloading and installing it.

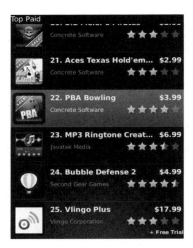

FIGURE 6-3 To work through this exercise, choose an app that you have to pay for.

To pay for and download an item from the App Store:

1. Locate the item by browsing or searching for it. To browse Featured items, click the left and right arrows on the screen. (If you don't see anything here, try Top Paid.)
2. Click the item. See Figure 6-3.
3. If you like, read the reviews or view the screen shots, and then click Purchase.
4. Click OK and type your PayPal e-mail address and password. Press the Enter key and click Log In.

 Remember, if the screen goes dark, press the Escape or Menu key.

5. Click Buy Now.
6. Wait while the application is downloaded.
7. Click Run, Install, Yes, OK, and/or work through any required steps, if prompted.
8. Click the new app in the My World screen to run it.

 App World Sends You an E-mail

You'll receive an e-mail after purchasing an app from App World.

FIGURE 6-4   You'll find downloaded apps under Downloads; from there you can access options to move them.

Move an App to the Home Screen

You know that you can start and run an app from the App World icon via the My World button. That may be okay the first few times, but if you decide you want to use the application a lot, you may want a faster way to open it. You just might want it on your Home screen. If that's the case, you need to move it there.

To move an app to the Home screen:

1. On the Home screen, click Downloads.
2. Tap the icon for the app one time, shown in Figure 6-4, and press the Menu key.
3. After clicking the Menu key, press Move to Folder, and click Home. The new application will appear on your Home screen and will no longer appear in the Downloads folder.

Use and Review an App

If you've been following along, you know that after installing an app, you can click it in My World and click Run to start the program. If you moved the icon for the app to the Home screen as detailed in the previous section, click it there. All you have to do now to get started playing with or using the app is to follow the directions given the first time you use it.

Write a Review of an Application

If you really enjoy an app, really hate it, or are even on the fence, consider writing a review. Reviews help others decide if the app is worth the time to download, the space required to install, and the price, if applicable. The easiest way to write a review is from the App World icon, and the My World screen inside it.

To write a review of an app:

1. On the BlackBerry menu screen, click App World.
2. In App World, click the My World button.
3. Click the program to review.
4. Click Reviews.
5. Click Add Review.
6. Select a rating, type a title, and write your review.
7. Click the Menu key and from the list, click Submit.

Contact a Vendor

All applications from the BlackBerry App World store have information related to the creator or vendor of the application. If you have a problem with the application, want to learn more about it, or want to see what other applications that particular vendor offers, you can contact the vendor or the vendor's web site.

To contact a vendor:

1. Open App World and click My World.
2. Click the application.
3. Scroll down to the bottom of the screen and click Contact Support or Contact Vendor. See Figure 6-5.
4. Type your question or comment, and then press the Mail icon in the top-right corner to send.

FIGURE 6-5 All apps have a way to contact the vendor or get support.

Remove an App

You may have gone a little crazy when you first started with apps. You surely have apps you no longer want. While the method for uninstalling applications isn't intuitive (you don't do it from App World or My World), it can be done. You just have to know how.

To remove an app from your phone:

1. On the BlackBerry menu screen, click Options.
2. In the Options screen, click Applications.
3. Click the application to remove.
4. From the resulting page, click Delete. You'll have to click Delete again to verify.

Some apps require you to reboot the phone to complete the deletion process.

Apps that are downloaded are stored in the phone's memory, not on the microSD card. Keep an eye on your internal memory if you download a lot of applications.

PART III

E-mail and the Internet

7

Set Up and Use E-mail

HOW TO...

- Distinguish among e-mail options
- Create a new BlackBerry e-mail address
- Add an existing e-mail account
- Send an e-mail to yourself to test settings
- Read an e-mail
- Reply to or forward an e-mail
- Delete an e-mail
- Attach a file to an e-mail
- Open an attachment
- Save an attachment
- Add a contact
- Move e-mail to a folder

Your BlackBerry offers access to your e-mail, including your personal and work e-mail. You can also set up a free BlackBerry e-mail if you like. In fact, you can configure up to ten e-mail accounts. You can set up your e-mail directly from the phone or using a desktop computer.

Once you have your account(s) set up on your BlackBerry, you can then start to receive, send, and reply to e-mail. As you acquire e-mail, you'll also need to manage it, including moving e-mail you want to save to folders, and you'll probably want to change some of the default settings for reading, saving, or deleting e-mail.

Set Up E-mail

If you've used a BlackBerry before and are familiar with it, you may have skipped right to this chapter after getting the book. You want to set up your home and work e-mail addresses and get moving; that's OK. In this section, you can dive right in, without having read any other part of the book.

In this first section, you'll learn how to distinguish among e-mail setup options first, because you may want to use an existing e-mail account, set up a new BlackBerry e-mail account, and/or set up and use an e-mail account from a specific provider, like Gmail or Hotmail. You may even have a corporate e-mail account you want to use. There are a lot of options.

Distinguish Among E-mail Options

There are all kinds of ways to get e-mail on your BlackBerry. Most BlackBerry users configure a personal e-mail account. You most likely have a personal e-mail address that you use at home to send and receive e-mail. Personal e-mail addresses are those that end in hotmail.com, gmail.com, comcast.net, verizon.net, and so on. One of my e-mail addresses is Joli_Ballew@hotmail.com.

You can also opt to acquire a free BlackBerry e-mail account. E-mail from a BlackBerry address shows up instantly on your phone, often only a few seconds after being sent, while e-mail from personal e-mail accounts comes in a little more slowly. However, BlackBerry Internet Service now offers almost real-time delivery of some accounts, including Hotmail, Gmail, Yahoo, and AOL, so if you're used to the 15-minute lag time, you're in for a nice surprise. If you want to get e-mail fast, opt for a BlackBerry e-mail address and ask your contacts to use it.

If you don't want to set up your personal accounts on your BlackBerry, you can configure e-mail forwarding. You can configure your home PC to check for e-mail every one or two minutes, and forward everything that comes in to your BlackBerry address. You do this by creating "rules" inside your mail program. Figure 7-1 shows an example of how you can create such a rule in Microsoft Outlook 2007. E-mail that is forwarded to your BlackBerry address will show up right away on your phone. This takes a little more work on your part, but can be exactly what is needed in certain circumstances.

 If you want to forward e-mail from a corporate account, you can talk to your network administrator at work about installing and configuring BlackBerry Redirector Software. There are some requirements, though, like associating your phone with Outlook, and having an Exchange or Enterprise Server. I won't cover that here; most readers won't have this at home, and will have an administrator to guide them at work.

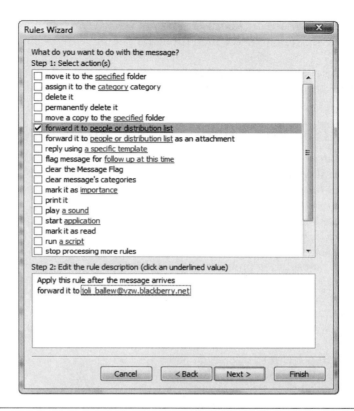

FIGURE 7-1   Although there will be issues when forwarding all mail from your home PC, it is possible with "rules."

 If you choose to forward e-mail that comes in on your home PC to your BlackBerry e-mail address, you'll have to leave the home PC on 24 hours a day. If the PC shuts down, turns off, reboots and requires a login, or the battery dies, it won't be able to forward e-mail.

There are a few other options. There's the option of third-party software, like Gmail Mobile, which acts as a separate e-mail client on your BlackBerry. You may opt for something like this if you want to keep your personal e-mail separate from your business e-mail. Because these are third-party applications, they won't be discussed here.

Of course, there are corporate e-mail accounts. These are e-mail addresses you use in a large company, generally for work purposes only. If you have a corporate account and want to synchronize your phone with the software you use at work, such as Microsoft Outlook, IBM Lotus Notes, or Novell GroupWise, and if your company has a BlackBerry Enterprise Server that you are allowed to associate your phone with, you can configure this on your BlackBerry as well. This is much less common than the former option, because there are many more people with personal e-mail addresses and a BlackBerry than there are people with corporate ones.

To set up a corporate account, you'll need to contact your network administrator for the required credentials. (Ask for the enterprise activation password.)

Create a New BlackBerry E-mail Address

A BlackBerry e-mail address is in the form < yourname >@< carrier >.blackberry.net. The advantage to having a BlackBerry address is that e-mail sent to that address is delivered instantly to your BlackBerry. If you need your e-mail fast, consider a free BlackBerry e-mail address.

In this section, you'll learn how to create a new BlackBerry e-mail address from your phone. You can also create your new address from any PC using the BlackBerry Internet Service. While creating the account from your phone almost always goes smoothly, sometimes problems do arise. For this reason, Verizon suggests you create the account from a computer. Directions for accessing the BlackBerry Internet Service web page are included in Chapter 8. If you're a "Safety Sadie," you can put off this task until the next chapter.

To create and configure a new BlackBerry e-mail address on your phone:

1. From the Home screen, click Setup.
2. Click E-mail Settings.
3. Click Add.
4. Click Create New Address.
5. Type the user name you'd like to use. Often, this is a company name, your name, your name with symbols, or your name followed by a number. See Figure 7-2.
6. Type a password that is at least six characters long and retype it to confirm. You will have to scroll through the screen to see these entries.
7. Select a secret question, type the answer, and click Next.
8. You'll be informed if your user name and other data is correct. If it is not, retype the required information. Click OK.

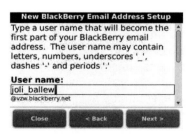

FIGURE 7-2   Type the user name you'd prefer. It may or may not be available.

Add an Existing Personal E-mail Account

If you choose to use a personal e-mail account that you already have, it's easy to set up. There's built-in support for certain web-based e-mail accounts, including:

- AOL Mail
- Windows Live
- Gmail
- Yahoo! Mail

If you have one of these accounts, setup is a breeze. Your BlackBerry knows the settings, so you don't have to input anything but your e-mail address and password. If you don't have one of these accounts, during setup, you'll have to click Other. From there, you can configure e-mail accounts obtained from Internet Service Providers (ISPs) like Time Warner, Verizon, AT&T, Comcast, COX, and more. During setup, you'll be required to populate the required fields with information you've obtained from your ISP. (Call your ISP if you aren't sure of the settings, or perform a web search for your ISP's "server settings.")

To configure a personal e-mail account:

1. From the Home screen, click Setup.
2. Click E-mail Settings.
3. Click Add.
4. If your e-mail account type is listed (Yahoo, Gmail, Live Mail, and so forth), click it. See Figure 7-3. Then:
   a. Type your e-mail address and password.
   b. Click Next.

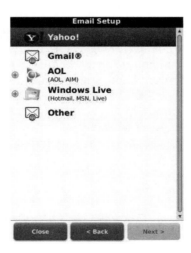

FIGURE 7-3   If your e-mail type is shown, click it.

    c. Click OK when you see your account has been set up properly. If there's an error message, follow the instructions to resolve it.

  5. If your e-mail account is not listed, click Other. Then:

    a. Type your e-mail address and password.

    b. Click Next.

    c. If prompted, input any additional information or resolve any error messages.

    d. Click OK.

  6. Continue adding e-mail addresses as required. You can see all addresses on the E-mail Accounts page.

Get to Know the Account Icons and Send an E-mail to Yourself to Test Settings

After you've set up your e-mail accounts, take a look at the Home screen. You'll see new icons for each account you created plus a generic "Messages" icon. If you created four e-mail accounts, you should see four icons (one for each account), and a fifth icon named Messages. To view messages from a specific account, click its icon. To view all messages from all accounts, click Messages.

 It's nice when all of your e-mail account icons are grouped together on the first line or two. If your accounts aren't grouped together on the Home screen, reposition them. See Chapter 4 for more information about repositioning icons.

While the default Home screen icons may suit you for a while, you may find after a while that you read e-mail using the Messages icon rather than clicking each individual account icon. You may prefer it for reading messages. If this becomes the case, consider hiding the unwanted icons. Refer to Chapter 4 if you need information on how to do that.

Once your e-mail accounts are set up on the BlackBerry, you should send yourself a test e-mail. Send an e-mail from each e-mail address you added back to the same address. If you can send and receive without errors, e-mail is set up correctly. The best way to do this is to send a message by clicking each e-mail icon, and returning there to verify it was received.

 If you opted for e-mail forwarding, send an e-mail to the address you've forwarded and verify the e-mail appears in your BlackBerry inbox.

To send a test e-mail from any configured account back to that same account:

  1. On the Home screen, note the top line. Click the first e-mail account icon. Do not click Messages.

  2. Click the Compose button in the bottom-left corner of the screen, as shown in the following illustration.

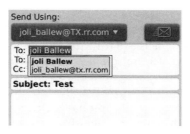

FIGURE 7-4   Enter your own contact name, complete the message, and click the Mail icon to send it.

3. Click E-mail. (You'll see other options including PIN, SMS Text, MMS, and Instant Message.)
4. Note the Send Using window. In the To line, type that address. See Figure 7-4.
5. Click the Mail icon to send it.
6. In a few minutes, check to see if the message arrived.

 If you receive an error message, something about your e-mail address isn't set up properly. If that happens, click Setup, E-mail Settings, select the problematic account, and review your user name, password, and other settings.

Send and Receive E-mail

Now that your e-mail is set up, you can start to send and receive e-mail. Although you'd think sending and receiving e-mail would be simple, and that there's really nothing left to learn that you don't already know, you'll be surprised to find out there's a lot more to e-mailing with your BlackBerry than you think.

For instance, you can read, reply, forward, and delete an e-mail with minimal clicking, and you can save and store e-mail you want to keep in another folder for safekeeping. You can even add attachments to outgoing e-mails. And once you get used to e-mailing from your BlackBerry, you'll discover there are many keyboard shortcuts, acronyms, and other ways you can e-mail more quickly and efficiently. Let's start by reading and replying to e-mail.

 Configure Sounds for E-mail

You can configure a sound to play when an e-mail arrives. From the Sounds icon, click Set Ring Tones/Alerts, and click Messages to get started.

Read an E-mail

When you have a new message (or multiple messages), you'll see a star on the Messages icon on your Home screen, as well as on the icon for the e-mail account. Click the related (starred) icon to read your mail. In addition to the red stars, you'll see a mail icon with a number by it at the top of the screen. The number represents how many new, unread e-mails you have. Once you click a starred icon to access the e-mail in it, the star disappears. Each time you read an e-mail (or receive a new one), the number changes at the top of the screen.

To read e-mail:

1. Click any icon with a star by it. That means that account has unread e-mail.
2. Click any e-mail to read it. See Figure 7-5.

  Use the up and down arrow keys to move through a list of e-mails or to scroll through the body of an e-mail that is longer than a screen.

Reply To or Forward an E-mail

After you've read an e-mail, you may want or need to reply to the sender with a message of your own, or you may want to forward the e-mail to someone else. Click Reply to send a response to the person who sent you the e-mail; click Forward to send the message to someone else.

FIGURE 7-5   If you're following along, you'll have a "Test" e-mail in each of your e-mail accounts.

Click Reply to All only when you want to send a response to everyone the e-mail was addressed to. Be careful that you do not click Reply To All unless you really do mean to send the response to everyone. (Reply to All won't appear as an option if you were the only person to whom the message was sent.)

To reply to or forward an e-mail:

1. Open an e-mail.
2. Click the leftmost icon to reply to a message (it has a green arrow pointing left); click the second icon to forward it (it has a blue icon pointing right).
3. Compose the message and click the Mail icon to send it.

Press the Escape key to return to the previous screen.

Delete an E-mail

Most of the time you'll want to delete e-mail soon after reading and answering it. You may want to keep an e-mail for a while if it has directions or a time and place in it, as a reminder, but you'll want to strive to keep your inbox and your BlackBerry as clean as possible.

To delete an e-mail after reading it:

- In a message, press the Menu key and click Delete. Click On Handheld, or click On Mailbox and Handheld.
- In the message list, press the Delete button. Click On Handheld, or click On Mailbox and Handheld.
- To delete multiple messages, touch the first message and the last message in a screen to select all messages in between. Click Delete. Click On Handheld, or click On Mailbox and Handheld.
- To delete messages prior to a specific date, in the message list, tap a horizontal date line. Press the Menu key and click Delete Prior. Click Delete to confirm.

If you opt for Delete On Mailbox and Handheld, you're also deleting the message on the e-mail server.

Attach a File to an E-mail

You can attach a file to an e-mail on your home or office PC by clicking Attach or Insert, and you can do the same on your BlackBerry. On a BlackBerry, you can attach a Microsoft Office document, pictures, music, and videos. You may want to attach a file you've edited, a picture that's on your phone, or even a spreadsheet or presentation.

To add an attachment to an e-mail:

1. Create a new e-mail from the Messages icon.
2. Compose the e-mail, adding a contact, subject, and body, and then click the Menu button and click Attach File. See Figure 7-6. Note that you can also opt to Attach Contact, which attaches a contact file.
3. Locate the item to attach.
4. Click the Mail icon to send the e-mail.

Open an Attachment

When someone sends you an e-mail with an attachment, you'll need to open the attachment to view it. You can view several attachment types including .zip, .htm, .jsp, .doc, .dot, .ppt, .pdf, .wpd, .txt, .vcf, and .xls files. You can also view .bmp, .gif, .jpg, .png, .tif, and .wmf files, and play .wav and .mp3 files.

 If you save an e-mail message that contains an attachment, both the e-mail message and the attachment are stored in the device memory.

To open an attachment:

1. In a message, click the attachment. You'll see the attachment at the top of the e-mail and in the body.
2. When you click the attachment you'll have the option Open Attachment. Click Open Attachment.
3. Click View. As shown in Figure 7-7, you may also see an editing option. If you choose to edit the document with Documents To Go, you'll have to accept the terms of service and use the Menu button to access the editing tools.

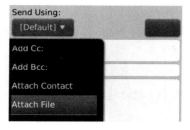

FIGURE 7-6   Attach File is an option from the Menu button while composing an e-mail.

View Tracked Changes in a Document

You can view tracked changes in a document by pressing the Menu key and selecting Show Changes.

Save an Attachment

Sometimes you'll get an e-mail that contains an attachment you want to keep, perhaps one that contains a funny video, a receipt, contact information, or the like. The specific steps for saving data to your BlackBerry are determined by the type of data you want to save, but for the most part, you'll open the data to view it, and then opt to save it using the choices under the Menu key. You can save pictures, videos, documents, and even entire e-mails.

To save data that's an attachment, such as a photo or video:

1. Locate the message that contains the attachment, click it, and click Open Attachment.
2. Click the Menu key. If the attachment is an image, click Save Image. Options will differ depending on the type of data to save.
3. By default, a picture will save to the Pictures folder, and documents will save to the Documents folder, videos to the Videos folder, and so on. If the folder that's showing is the one you want, click Save. If you want to save to another folder:
   a. Click the Folder icon.
   b. Click a folder to save to.

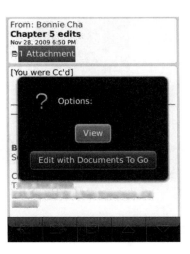

FIGURE 7-7 You can view most attachments, and some you can edit.

c. Click Select Folder when prompted.
d. Click Save.

You can rename any attachment by clicking the name during the save process. A window will appear where you can use the keyboard to type a new name for the file.

Add a Contact

When you receive an e-mail from a person who is not currently in your contact list, you may want to add them. The simplest way to do this is to:

1. Open the message.
2. Click the Menu key.
3. Click Add to Contacts. See Figure 7-8.

To add the contact to your Contacts list while reading an e-mail, click the Menu key and click Add to Contacts.

FIGURE 7-8 Add to Contacts is an option from the Menu key.

8

Explore Advanced
E-mail Options

HOW TO...

- Log on to the BlackBerry Internet Service web site
- Create an e-mail filter
- Delete an e-mail filter
- Create and add a signature
- Check spelling before sending an e-mail
- Request a read or delivery receipt
- Stop loading pictures in e-mails
- Shorten how much of an e-mail you receive
- Edit e-mail account settings

Once you've set up your e-mail accounts and worked a little with your BlackBerry, you'll find you want to do a little tweaking. You may want to create an e-mail filter to manage incoming mail, set options so that the BlackBerry checks the spelling of outgoing e-mail before you send it, set an out-of-office reply, and more. You can also improve e-mail performance by making changes such as disabling pictures in e-mails, or limit how much of an e-mail is downloaded. Making these changes can enhance your mail experience, and make your BlackBerry easier to use and manage.

Filter E-mail

You have the power to decide what e-mail is delivered to your BlackBerry and what is not. You may only want to receive e-mail from work, for instance, or you may only want to receive e-mail from friends and family. Additionally, you may have a few people you do not want to receive mail from, like a mail list or a specific mail group.

To configure who you do and don't receive mail from, create e-mail message filters using the BlackBerry Internet Service (BIS) web site, created by the company Research in Motion, but provisioned by your service provider (likely Verizon). When creating a filter, you can state what should be received on your BlackBerry based on who sent the e-mail, who it was sent to, and/or what level of importance the sender assigned to the e-mail message, if any. (You may always want to receive e-mail assigned High Priority from everyone.)

 When multiple filters are assigned, they are applied based on the order in which they appear in the filter list.

Here are some of the ways you can filter messages:

- **From**   You can specify the contacts and mail addresses you want to receive mail from based on what appears in the From line of the incoming e-mail.
- **CC to me**   You can specify if you want to receive mail when you are listed in the CC field.
- **High Priority**   You can specify that all high-priority e-mail should be sent to your phone.
- **To**   You can specify the contacts and mail addresses you want to receive mail from based on what appears in the To line of the incoming e-mail.

 When you create a filter with multiple contacts, separate them with a semicolon.

Log On to the BlackBerry Internet Web Site

If you receive unwanted e-mail on your BlackBerry, you can create a filter to stop it from arriving. You may belong to an e-mail list or a web community, for instance, or some other Internet-related group that creates a lot of e-mails you really don't need to receive on your phone. You may not want to receive e-mail from your mother-in-law, for instance, but do want to receive e-mail from your own mom. You create the filters using a web browser on a computer. You'll have to locate the appropriate web site first, and then create a user name and password.

 Filtering e-mails from arriving on your phone does not stop them from arriving on your PC.

To locate the web site that offers access to the BlackBerry Internet Service for your provider, in any search engine on any computer, type **BlackBerry Internet Service** followed by your provider's name (perhaps **Verizon**). You're looking for something like what's shown in Figure 8-1.

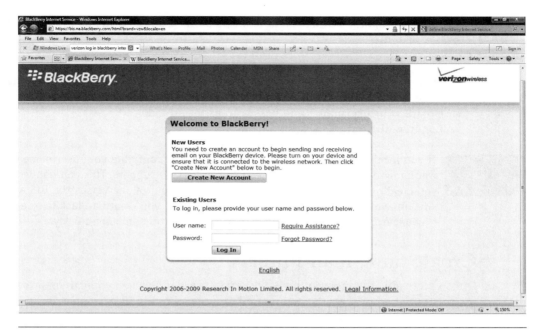

FIGURE 8-1   Locate the BlackBerry Internet Service web site provisioned by your service provider.

Once you've navigated to the site, you can sign in with your BlackBerry user name, which

- You may have created if and when you set up a BlackBerry e-mail address.
- You may have created when you worked through the setup wizards when you first got your phone.
- You may have never created.
- You may have created but do not remember creating it or the user name and/or password.

 Your BlackBerry user name is not your BlackBerry e-mail address, nor is it the name or password you applied to your phone.

To get a user name and password to access the BlackBerry Internet Service site, or to find out if you've already created one you've forgotten about:

1. At the BlackBerry Internet Service web site, input your PIN and Device ESN/ MEID, both of which you can find on your phone. To find this information:
   a. From the BlackBerry menu screen, click Options.
   b. Click Status.

You can find the PIN and MEID numbers on the outside of the box your BlackBerry arrived in.

2. Type the PIN and the MEID HEX number into the web page. If you receive an error, see the following note.
3. Create your user name and password as prompted.
4. Log in with your new user name and password.

 If you receive a message stating that you cannot configure your user name from a web browser on a PC, you will need to call Verizon support. This can happen when you create your BlackBerry e-mail address from your phone versus the BIS web site. To avoid this problem, Verizon suggests that you create a BlackBerry e-mail account from a PC. Dial 800-922-0204 to resolve this problem quickly.

Create an E-mail Filter

Once you're able to log on to the BlackBerry Internet Service, you can create a filter for any e-mail address you've configured on your phone.

To create a filter using a web browser:

1. In the BlackBerry Internet Service web site, log in and in the left pane, click E-mail Accounts. See Figure 8-2.
2. Click the Filters icon next to any e-mail address, as shown in the following illustration.
3. Click Add a Filter.
4. Type a filter name.
5. In the Apply Filter When drop-down list, select a filter.
6. If prompted, type additional information, like an e-mail address to define the sender to whom the filter should be applied. See Figure 8-3.
7. Select the notification options and click Add Filter.

 As long as you're here, configure as many filters as you can think of. Consider all of the unwanted e-mail you get, and add filters to minimize it.

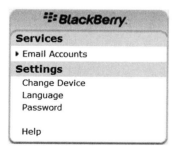

FIGURE 8-2   One of the options after logging in is to configure your e-mail accounts.

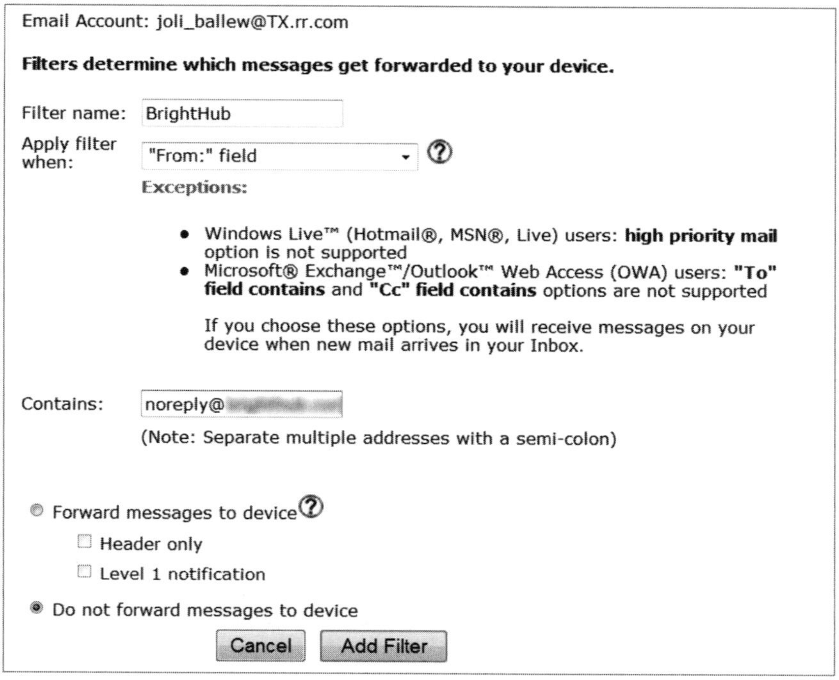

Email Account: joli_ballew@TX.rr.com

Filters determine which messages get forwarded to your device.

Filter name: BrightHub

Apply filter when: "From:" field   ▾   ②

Exceptions:

- Windows Live™ (Hotmail®, MSN®, Live) users: **high priority mail** option is not supported
- Microsoft® Exchange™/Outlook™ Web Access (OWA) users: **"To" field contains** and **"Cc" field contains** options are not supported

If you choose these options, you will receive messages on your device when new mail arrives in your Inbox.

Contains: noreply@ ▓▓▓▓▓▓▓ ▓▓▓

(Note: Separate multiple addresses with a semi-colon)

◎ Forward messages to device②
   ☐ Header only
   ☐ Level 1 notification
◉ Do not forward messages to device

[Cancel]   [Add Filter]

FIGURE 8-3   Configure filter options to keep unwanted e-mail from being delivered to your BlackBerry.

Delete an E-mail Filter

If you create a filter and decide you no longer need or want it, you can delete it. To delete an e-mail filter:

1. Log in to the BlackBerry Internet Service web site.
2. Click the Filter icon to access the filters already created.
3. Click Delete next to the filter you no longer want or need.

Did You Know?

Filter Limitations

You can only create filters for e-mail addresses that appear in BIS. If you use a third-party application to retrieve e-mail from the web, those addresses won't appear here.

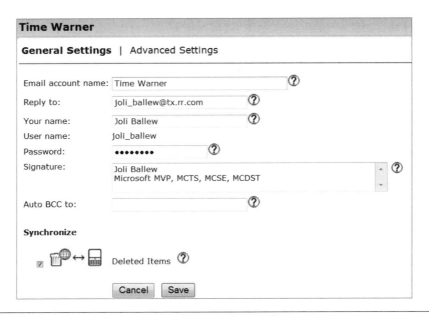

FIGURE 8-4   Create a signature you like, and consider renaming your account.

Create, Add, or Edit a Signature

A signature appears at the end of e-mail messages that you send from your phone. By default, that signature is *Sent from my Verizon Wireless BlackBerry*. You can replace the signature with one of your own, or delete the signature entirely. To edit the signature or create your own, log in to the BlackBerry Internet Service web site using any web browser and click the Edit icon.

To create, edit, or add a signature using a web browser:

1. In a browser on your computer, go to the BlackBerry Internet Service web site, and in the left pane, click E-mail Accounts.
2. Click the Edit icon beside an e-mail address.
3. In the Signature field, type a signature. Review the additional options. You may want to change your e-mail account name for instance, or apply synchronization options. Click the ? sign if you are unsure what any field represents. See Figure 8-4.
4. Click Save.

Did You Know?

Changes Are Applied Automatically

You can change the e-mail account name on the BIS, and the change will automatically appear on your BlackBerry phone.

Enhance Your E-mail

You can enhance the e-mail you send in a number of ways. One way is to make sure it's readable and contains no spelling errors. There's an option you can enable to check spelling prior to sending the message. This works pretty well, but like anything else, it can be a time-waster if you use acronyms or other "words" that the spell check application doesn't recognize.

In addition to spell check, you can configure an out-of-office reply to be sent to people who e-mail you when you're on vacation or will be away for a few days. A reply like this can be set to tell people how long you'll be away and when they might expect a response.

 You can only set an out-of-office reply if you use an Enterprise server or a BlackBerry Professional server. If you have this, to configure a reply, click Options, click E-mail Settings, and set Out Of Office Reply to Yes.

Although it's certainly not the last of the options you can configure, you can also ask for a read or delivery receipt if you need verification that a message was delivered or read (or selected in the recipient's inbox).

Check Spelling Before Sending an E-mail

If you would like your BlackBerry to check the spelling in your e-mails prior to sending them, you can enable Spell Check. If there are misspelled words, you'll have a chance to correct them before the e-mail is sent.

To enable Spell Check:

1. On the BlackBerry menu screen, click Options.
2. In Options, click Spell Check.
3. Select the Spell Check E-mail Before Sending option.
4. Press the Menu key.
5. Click Save.

Request a Read or Delivery Receipt

When you send an e-mail, you do not know when the e-mail was delivered or when it was read. By default, you aren't notified. You can configure any message you send

 More about Spell Check

You can add words to the Spell Check feature by adding new words to the Custom Dictionary. Click Custom Dictionary in Step 3, click the Menu key, and click New to add your own entries.

FIGURE 8-5   Configure notifications appropriately if you want to receive delivery or read receipts.

so that you are informed when a message is delivered to its intended recipient and/ or when the recipient clicked the message in their inbox to read it. These are called delivery and read receipts.

 A read receipt only notifies you that the person clicked the message in their inbox, presumably to read it. However, there's no guarantee the recipient actually read the e-mail, only that they clicked it.

To request a read or delivery receipt:

1. Click an icon on the Home screen that represents one of your e-mail accounts.
2. Press the Menu key and click Options.
3. Click E-mail Settings.
4. If necessary, change the account in the Message Services field.
5. To request delivery or read notifications, change the Confirm Delivery and Confirm Read fields. See Figure 8-5.

 The final option on the E-mail Settings screen is Send Read Receipts. It's set to No, meaning that your phone will not automatically send Read receipts if the sender requests it. To automatically send Read receipts, change this field from No to Yes.

6. Press the Menu key.
7. Click Save.

Improve Performance

If you want to improve the performance of e-mail on your BlackBerry, you can make changes to the default settings. For instance, by default, pictures inside e-mails load when you read an e-mail. Pictures take a long time to load, so if you'd like to speed things along, you can opt to not load pictures in e-mails. If later it turns out you really do want to see a picture in a specific e-mail, you can load only the pictures in that particular message.

You can also shorten how much of an e-mail you receive, opting to view more of the e-mail if you deem it important. This will improve performance by limiting how much of an e-mail is loaded when the entire e-mail isn't actually necessary.

Finally, you can stop forwarding messages to your BlackBerry to discontinue mail from coming in from accounts you don't use, don't want to hear from, or that only offer Spam and unwanted e-mail you don't need to read.

 If you're still getting too much mail after working through this section, return to the filtering section in this chapter to reduce the total amount of mail you receive.

Stop Loading Pictures in E-mails

You can opt to not load pictures that come attached to e-mails. Doing so will cause the e-mail to be downloaded to your phone more quickly and thus, enhance performance. Much of the time, especially with e-mail that comes from web sites like Amazon.com or Microsoft, images that are included with the message aren't important. For instance, if you are expecting a receipt from Amazon, you don't need to see the Amazon logo at the top of the page to understand what the e-mail is all about.

If you decide to stop loading pictures in e-mails and then receive an e-mail that contains pictures you want to see, you can enable pictures in that e-mail only. Just click Menu and Get Images.

To stop loading images inside e-mail you receive:

1. On the Home screen, click any e-mail account icon.
2. Click the Menu key and click Options.
3. Click E-mail Settings.
4. If necessary, change the Message Services field.
5. Change the Download Images Automatically field to No.
6. Press the Menu key.
7. Click Save.

 To view pictures in any HTML e-mail, press the Menu key and click Get Images.

Shorten How Much of an E-mail You Receive

When you receive an e-mail on your BlackBerry, the entire message is downloaded. If the message is long, it may take a second or more to download it. If you don't want to load the entire message, you can only load the first part of it. If you decide the message is worth reading after looking at the first few lines, you can click More to read the rest. This will improve how fast e-mail is received on your BlackBerry.

To limit how much of a message is loaded:

1. On the Home screen, click any message icon.
2. Click the Menu key and click Options.
3. Click General Options.
4. Change the Auto More field to No.
5. Press the Menu key.
6. Click Save.

 Consider turning off confirmation for deleting e-mails and/or how long to keep e-mails before automatically deleting them.

Edit E-mail Account Settings

If you cannot get your messages from a specific e-mail account, you may have input incorrect information in your e-mail account settings during setup. You can return to the e-mail account settings to repair this, or to configure or browse advanced settings. If there's nothing wrong with your e-mail, though, there's likely no reason to go mucking about in here. However, if you are still not getting the performance you want, you can certainly try to tweak the settings here.

To change advanced e-mail account settings:

1. From a PC, navigate to the BlackBerry Internet Service web site, and in the left pane, click E-mail Accounts.
2. Click the Edit icon beside a POP or IMAP e-mail address.
3. Click Advanced Settings. View the information there. Phone your ISP for the e-mail account and ask what settings should be input here.
4. Change the advanced options for your e-mail address if required.
5. Click Save.

You can also make changes to your account using your BlackBerry:

1. On the Home screen, click the Messages icon for the account to configure.
2. Click the Menu key and click Options.
3. Click E-mail Reconciliation. For On Conflicts, verify that Mailbox Wins is selected. That's the default. Verify that the settings for Wireless Reconcile are On. See Figure 8-6.
4. If you made changes, click the Menu key and click Save.

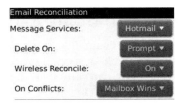

FIGURE 8-6   If you're having problems with your e-mail, check the advanced settings.

9

Explore Internet and Browser Basics

HOW TO...

- Visit a web page
- Save a web page
- Search the Internet
- Find a word on a web page
- Zoom in on a web page
- Click a link in a web page
- View browsing history
- Copy and/or send a web page address
- Play media on a web page
- Switch browser views
- Set a Home page
- Add a bookmark for a web page
- View and access bookmarks
- Delete a bookmark
- Move a bookmark
- Rename a bookmark
- Create a subfolder for bookmarks
- Change display options
- Clear Cache and History
- Configure browser push

Your BlackBerry offers always-on access to the Internet. You can visit any web page you like, click links, and otherwise browse the web almost as you would on your PC or Mac. Browsing with a BlackBerry might be a little slower than you're used to, though, and it may not have all the perks (like Flash support), but all in all, it's a satisfying experience.

There's more to surfing the Internet than clicking through web pages, though. With your BlackBerry, you can view online media, send links to others, and manage myriad bookmarks. You can also do many of the things you're familiar with on a desktop computer, including setting a Home page and viewing browsing history. In this chapter, you'll learn how to do all of this and more.

 In this chapter, I assume that you have an unlimited data plan and do not need to worry about how much bandwidth you use during your Internet sessions.

Browse and Search the Internet

Surfing through web pages is the most basic Internet-related activity there is. You type in a web address or navigate to a web page, scan or read the page, and click links included in the page to get to other pages. You can also type search words in a Search box to get results and links to other pages, and you can return to your browsing history if you want to visit a place you've already been. You can also access your bookmarks to quickly mark and go to pages you visit often. These are basic tasks, likely something you do quite often on your desktop computer.

Performing the tasks on a BlackBerry is almost the same as using a desktop computer, at least in theory. To surf the Internet on a BlackBerry, you open a web browser and navigate to the page you want to view by typing or searching, or choosing from saved bookmarks. Just as on a computer, though, there's more you can do than that. While surfing, you can save a web page, play media on a page, look for a specific word on a page, and more. And that's just the beginning!

Visit a Web Page

You can visit a web page in several ways, one of which is to type in the web address or URL (Uniform Resource Locator). After you've visited some pages and saved some bookmarks, you can access those pages again from your History and Bookmarks list. You can also move from one page to another by clicking links in a page.

To visit a web page by typing in its address:

1. On the BlackBerry menu screen, click Browser.

 Unless otherwise noted, everything in this chapter starts by clicking Browser or being in the browser application.

FIGURE 9-1 Type the address for the web page.

2. If you see an address field where you can type a web address as shown in Figure 9-1, you're ready to go; skip to Step 3. If you don't see the address field, click the Menu key and click Go To.
3. Click in the address field after http://www. and type the name of the web site you'd like to visit. See Figure 9-1.
4. Click Go.
5. Once you're on any web page, click a link to go to another page, type a keyword into the Search box (more on this later), or click the Escape key to return to the previous page

 Use the Zoom In and Zoom Out buttons on the phone to get a better look at what's on the web page. Use your finger to scroll through the page after zooming in on it, or simply lightly double-tap to zoom in.

Save a Web Page

You may want to save a web page for future reference. Saving a web page is not the same as creating a bookmark for it, though. Saving the web page really just creates a picture of it in its current state. You can save a page that contains information you'd like to refer to later.

To save a web page:

1. On any web page, press the Menu key.
2. Click Save Page.
3. Note that you can change the name of the page and that it will be saved in your Message list. Click OK. See Figure 9-2.
4. When you're ready to view the site, simply go to your Message Inbox and select the saved web page.

FIGURE 9-2   When you save a web page, it appears in your Message list.

Search the Internet

You may not always know what web page you want to visit. You may need to search for the appropriate page or seek out specific information using a keyword search. When you want to find information on the Internet by searching for it, you have to type in your search words and peruse the results.

To search for something on the Internet:

1. On the BlackBerry menu screen, click Browser.
2. If you see an address field where you can type a web address, skip to Step 3. If you don't see the address field, click the Menu key and click Go To.
3. In the window under the Address field, in the Search field, click and then type your keywords.
4. Press Enter.
5. If you prefer another search engine over Google for your next search, click the blue search engine icon next to the Search window (not shown). You can choose from Live Search, Wikipedia, and Dictionary.com, as shown in Figure 9-3.

FIGURE 9-3   There are four built-in search engines.

Find a Word on a Web Page

Sometimes you'll need to locate a specific word on a web page. Perhaps you searched for a specific keyword using the Search window on a web page, then navigated to the page that contains that word, and now need to locate the word on the page.

To find a specific word on a web page (the following method also works for an e-mail message or attachment):

1. Press the Menu key.
2. Click Find.
3. Type the text you'd like to search for and press the Enter key.
4. The browser will then take you to the point on the page where the search term appears or displays a Not Found message if there are no results.

Zoom In on a Web Page

The BlackBerry browser will often default to the mobile-optimized version of a site (for example, CNN, NY Times) when it's available; however, many web pages aren't optimized or created for extremely small screens like the one on your BlackBerry. Most web pages are meant to be viewed on computer monitors. On a larger screen, just about any web page is easy to see and to read. When you visit one of these "regular" pages on your BlackBerry, the text will be so small you won't be able to read it. You'll need to be able to zoom in to see the page more clearly.

To zoom in on a web page, you can use one of these two methods:

- Quickly tap (but not press) the screen twice to zoom in. Press the Escape key to zoom out.
- Press the Zoom In icon on the screen to zoom in, and press the Zoom Out icon to zoom out.

 There are some web pages that are optimized for viewing on your BlackBerry. Facebook is an example. However, the Facebook mobile page does not include nearly as much information as the full site does, and you may decide it only works well enough to update your own status.

Click a Link in a Web Page

It's safe to say that virtually all web pages contain links to other web pages. That's how the Internet is connected, via web page links. Therefore, you can move through the Internet by clicking a link in one page to get to another.

To click a link in a web page:

1. In the browser, navigate to any web page.
2. Locate a link; links are generally blue.
3. Touch the link with your finger and press on the screen to go to the linked page.

View Browsing History

While browsing, you'll come across many web pages. Some you'll bookmark for future reference, and you may select one for your Home page (more on that later), but most of the pages you'll visit you won't save or mark for any future dealings with. It never fails, though—at some point you'll need to return to a page you visited but did not bookmark! When this happens, you can view a list of web pages you've recently visited. This list does not contain all of the pages you've ever visited, but it does hold the more recent ones.

To view a list of web pages you've recently visited on your BlackBerry:

1. On the BlackBerry menu screen, click the Browser icon.
2. Press the Menu key.
3. Click History.
4. Click a day if desired or applicable; click any page to go there. See Figure 9-4.

Copy and/or Send a Web Page Address

On occasion you'll visit a web page that you'd like to share. You may want to share the web address for your favorite restaurant, for a funny video on YouTube, or perhaps a link to a picture of a great pair of shoes. Whatever the case, it's possible to send a link on a web page to someone else. You can copy the address and paste it in a text or e-mail, or perhaps even a document, or you can send the web page address via e-mail, text, PIN, or other message option in a single step. Here you'll learn how to do both.

To copy the address for a web page you're currently visiting:

1. While you're at the web page, press the Menu key.
2. Click Page Address.

FIGURE 9-4 The History list offers a way to navigate to recently visited web pages.

3. Click Copy Address.
4. Now you can open an e-mail, and in the body of the e-mail press the Menu key again, and click Paste. You can also paste in various other applications, including texts and documents.

You can send a link for an *item* on a web page, too. Select the item with a tap; it may be a picture, link, or icon. Once the item is selected, click the Menu key and click Image Address, Link Address, or Page Address, as applicable.

You can send a web page address via text, e-mail, PIN, BlackBerry Messenger, and more, all from the Menu key. To send a web page address using this method:

1. On the BlackBerry menu screen, click the Browser icon.
2. On any web page, tap to select an item to share, and press the Menu key.
3. Click Send Address. See Figure 9-5.
4. Click a message type (E-mail, PIN, SMS Text, MMS, Messenger Contact). As applicable, finalize the message.

Play Media on a Web Page

Media is incorporated in many web pages. The media might be a video, a song, an animation, or something else. You can opt to play the media by clicking it. Note that not all media will play, though. If the media requires a component called "Flash," you won't be able to view it.

FIGURE 9-5   Send Address lets you send a web address quickly, without bothering with copying and pasting.

To play and/or save media on a web page:

1. In the browser on a web page that contains media; navigate to www.youtube.com, if desired.
2. Click any media file to play it.
3. Click the Escape button to return to the previous web page, if desired.

Personalize the Browser

You can personalize your web browser with bookmarks to your favorite web pages, a Home page, and a specific browser view. You can define the smallest font size to use in a web page or state that the fonts should be bold. And there's much more than this to explore. Configure all of these things together to get the most from your BlackBerry web browsing experience.

Switch Browser Views

There are two available browser views, Page and Column. You can change the view permanently from the Options for the browser, under General Properties. However, you may find it more useful to simply change the views when desired while on a web page.

To change the browser view while on a web page, click the Column View button (the second icon on the toolbar at the bottom of the screen) to go to Column view, or click the Page View button to go to Page view. It is a toggle and is either Column or Page. Page view is good for many web pages, but when the text and images are optimized for a computer monitor, Column view may be better.

If you decide you prefer one view over another and would like to set it as the default:

1. On the Home screen, click the Browser icon.
2. Press the Menu key.
3. Click Options.
4. Click General Properties.
5. Change the Default View field to the desired option.
6. Press the Menu key.
7. Click Save Options.

Open the Browser to a Home Page

When you open your browser, either the last page you opened appears, a Home page appears, or the BlackBerry's Start page appears. It depends on how your BlackBerry is configured. There are several ways to navigate to a new page from there:

- You can click the Menu key, click Go To, and click a bookmark;
- You can click the Escape key to go to the previously visited page;

- You can click the Menu key and click History or Recent Pages; or
- You can click the Menu key and Home to navigate to your "home" page.

A Home page is often your favorite web "starting point," perhaps Google, Live.com, or a similar page. A Home page may be configured on your BlackBerry already, but you can change it if it is. Once you've configured a Home page, you can tell your BlackBerry to always open the browser in that page, if you like. (If you don't want to do this, you can always click the Menu key and Home to get to your Home page quickly.)

To configure a Home page, first, navigate to the page you want to use:

1. On the Home screen, click the Browser icon.
2. Navigate to the page you'd like to use as your Home page.
3. Press the Menu key.
4. Click Options.
5. Click Browser Configuration.
6. At the bottom of the page, click Use Current. See Figure 9-6.

 If you want the Home page to open when you open the browser, next to Start Page, click Home Page.

7. Press the Menu key.
8. Click Save Options.

FIGURE 9-6   Navigate to a page you'd like to set as your Home page, and in Browser Configuration, click Use Current.

Add a Bookmark for a Web Page

You should add bookmarks for web pages that you visit regularly. That way, you can simply click the bookmark to revisit the page, versus searching for it or typing in the web address each time. When you add a bookmark, you are given the option to have the browser check the web page for updates periodically. You may want to configure this for web sites like Facebook, CNN, or a weather-related web site you visit regularly.

To add a bookmark for a web page:

1. In the browser on any web page, press the Menu key.
2. Click Add Bookmark.
3. In the Auto Synchronize field, set how often the browser should check for updates to the web page. See Figure 9-7.
4. In the Start Time field, set the time of day when the browser should start checking for updates. Click OK.
5. Click Add.

To change an existing bookmark:

1. On the Home screen, click the Browser icon.
2. Press the Menu key.
3. Click Bookmarks.
4. Highlight a bookmark.
5. Press the Menu key.

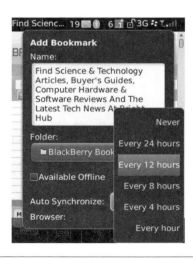

FIGURE 9-7 You can opt to have your BlackBerry browser check for updates to certain web pages automatically on a schedule.

6. Click Edit Bookmark.
7. Change the bookmark.
8. Click Save.

Use Bookmarks

There's a lot more to bookmarks than adding them so that you'll have easy access to them later. You can view them, delete them, rename them, and more. All of this falls under the category of managing your bookmarks. You'll have no bookmarks to manage until you add some, though, so if you don't have any bookmarks yet, return to the previous section to add some!

View and Access Bookmarks

To go to a web page you have already bookmarked, you'll need to click the Options button. There, you'll see Bookmarks, and you can click it to see a list of bookmarks. Scroll through the list to find the bookmark you want, and click it to go there.

   To view your bookmarks and then access a bookmarked web page:

1. In the web browser, click the Options button.
2. Click Bookmarks.
3. Click any bookmark to go there. You'll see the bookmarks you've configured under BlackBerry Bookmarks. You'll also see Links, among other things.

Manage Bookmarks

Once you've acquired some bookmarks, you'll find you occasionally need to manage them in one way or another. Perhaps you want to delete a bookmark you no longer use or send a bookmark to someone else. You may want to organize your personal bookmarks in subfolders or change the order of the bookmarks you've saved. You can do all of this and more from the Bookmarks options after pressing the Menu key.

 You can only manage bookmarks you've created, and they are listed in Bookmarks under BlackBerry Bookmarks. You won't find the same management options under Links, WAP Bookmarks, or Wi-Fi Services.

   To delete a bookmark:

1. On the Home screen, click the Browser icon.
2. Press the Menu key and click Bookmarks.
3. Look only in your BlackBerry bookmarks. You can only delete bookmarks you've created. See Figure 9-8.
4. Highlight a bookmark.
5. Press the Menu key and click Delete Bookmark. Delete again to confirm.

FIGURE 9-8 You can only manage bookmarks that are listed under BlackBerry Bookmarks.

To move a bookmark for a web page:

1. On the Home screen, click the Browser icon.
2. Press the Menu key and click Bookmarks.
3. Highlight a bookmark you've created and listed under BlackBerry Bookmarks, and press the Menu key.
4. Click Move Bookmark.
5. Tap, but do not press, the position in the list of bookmarks where this bookmark should be moved.

To rename a bookmark:

1. On the Home screen, click the Browser icon.
2. Click the Options button and click Bookmarks.
3. Highlight a bookmark you created.
4. Press the Menu key and click Edit Bookmark.
5. Click inside the Name field, click the back key on the keyboard to erase the current name, and use the keyboard to type a new one. As with any other typing task, your BlackBerry will suggest words for you.

FIGURE 9-9   Create subfolders under BlackBerry Bookmarks to organize your bookmarks.

To create a subfolder for bookmarks:

1. On the Home screen, click the Browser icon.
2. Click the Options button and click Bookmarks.
3. Tap BlackBerry Bookmarks to highlight it.
4. Press the Menu key and click Add Subfolder. If you don't see Add Subfolder, you've clicked a bookmark and not the BlackBerry Bookmarks root folder.
5. Type a name for the subfolder and click OK. See Figure 9-9.
6. You can now save or move bookmarks to the new subfolder, using techniques you've already learned.

Web Feeds

Web feeds provide you with updates to web site content as it changes. *If you can find a web site that contains a web feed and it's available so that you can view it on your BlackBerry*, you'll see additional options from the Options list, including Add Web Feed, Show Description, Get Audio, and Read Story. At the time this book was written, RSS feeds were fairly difficult to find.

If you do find an RSS feed to subscribe to, you'll manage feeds the same way you manage bookmarks. When you add a feed, you'll see a new root folder in the Bookmarks list entitled Web Feeds.

It is perhaps easier and more efficient to simply browse to a web site's RSS Feed page. For instance, you can navigate to www.espn.com and search for RSS. The results will take you to their News Feed Index, which you can bookmark and visit whenever you like.

Configure Browser Options

There are two ways to configure your browser. You can change browser options settings from the Options menu on the BlackBerry menu screen and from the Options menu within the browser. In this section, you'll explore both.

You can clear your browser history, so anyone snooping around in your phone can't see what web sites you've recently visited. You can opt not to show images at all, to increase the rate web pages load. You can change the minimum default size for fonts, the quality of images you view, and even opt to never view web page animations (or only let them repeat a specific number of times).

There are other options too, all of which you'll see when you start making configuration changes. Each option has a default setting that is optimal for most BlackBerry users. You'll find that default settings are set the way you'll probably want them too. For instance, the options for JavaScript, which allow you to interact with web pages more easily and effectively, are set for best performance. There are options to support JavaScript, allow JavaScript pop-ups, and to terminate slow-running scripts, and they are preconfigured with efficient settings. (You probably don't want to see pop-ups!) If you know about JavaScript, and you want to make changes, though, you certainly can. If you don't know anything about this, leave it be, but you know that even if you make a change, you can always change it back!

With all that said, here you'll learn how to access and make changes to the most common browser features, including changing how pictures and animations appear on a web page, clearing your browsing history, changing basic display settings, and clearing the cache, and configuring Push. (You'll learn more about the latter later in the chapter.)

To change how pictures and animations appear on a web page:

1. On the Home screen, click the Browser icon.
2. Press the Menu key and click Options.
3. Click Browser Configuration, then:
   - To stop displaying pictures, deselect Show Images.
   - To stop showing background images, deselect Use Background Images.
   - To disable support for embedded media, like music for instance, deselect Support Embedded Media.
4. Click the Escape key and click Save if prompted.
5. Click General Properties, then:
   - To change the number of times that animated graphics repeat, click 100 Times next to Repeat Animations and make a different selection.
   - To change the quality of the images shown on web pages, choose Low (Faster) or High (Slower) in Image Quality.
   - To change the minimum font size, select a new size next to Minimum Font Size.
   - To change the font style from Plain to Bold or Extra Bold, select the appropriate option next to Minimum Font Style.
6. Click the Escape key, and if prompted, click Save.

To clear browser history:

1. On the Home screen, click the Browser icon.
2. Press the Menu key and click Options.
3. Click Cache Operations.
4. Click Clear History.

Clear Cache

When you visit a web page, pictures, icons, and other data must be downloaded onto your BlackBerry. This takes some time. To make the process go more quickly, your web browser may save and store some of the data that's been downloaded in an area called the "cache." When you visit a web site the next time, your browser will check its cache to see if it's already downloaded any of the information on the page. If it has, it won't download it again; instead, it will pull it from the cache. This helps hasten the downloading and reloading of pages, because not all of the data has to be obtained again.

Cache folders can get quite large, though, and can occupy valuable hard drive space, perhaps by storing graphics for web sites you may never visit again. It's generally advised that you empty the cache periodically. Emptying the caches also forces the browser to obtain updated web data because the older cache items are no longer available and can't interfere.

To empty the cache on your BlackBerry:

1. On the Home screen, click the Browser icon.
2. Press the Menu key.
3. Click Options.
4. Click Cache Operations.
5. Beside Content Cache, click Clear.
6. Press the Escape key.

Configure Browser Push

Browser push allows your BlackBerry to *push* information from a web application to your phone as the information becomes available. For instance, you can use browser push to receive updates from a web application that have to do with changing weather reports, updated stock quotes, or late-breaking news. When updates are available and after they have been pushed to your phone, you may see a browser push message on the Home screen, or on an icon on your screen. You may not see anything at all; it depends on the web application. After information has been pushed to your device, it's on your device. You do not have to be connected to a wireless network to access the data.

FIGURE 9-10 Disable Push if you do not want to use it.

To enable or disable browser push:

1. On the Home screen or in a folder, click the Options icon.
2. Click Advanced Options and click Browser Push.
3. To disable all browser push messages, clear the Enable Push, Enable MDS Push, and Enable WAP Push check boxes. See Figure 9-10.
4. Press the Menu key.
5. Click Save.

10

Use Wi-Fi

The BlackBerry Storm2 can connect to and run on a variety of networks, but here in the United States it's the CDMA/EV-DO Rev-A network. The Storm2 can also connect to and run on Wi-Fi networks. (The first Storm could not.) Public Wi-Fi networks are often called "hotspots." Hotspots generally offer free access to the Internet, and are often available in local libraries, hotels, coffee shops, and cafes.

Your BlackBerry can also connect to private Wi-Fi networks. If you have a wireless network in your home, you can configure your BlackBerry to access it too. Many users swear by Wi-Fi, and claim they get faster and better Internet service when they use it, over what their service providers make available via mobile technologies. The immediate downside to Wi-Fi is the battery drain; with Wi-Fi turned on, your BlackBerry is constantly searching for networks and using additional battery power. The immediate upside to Wi-Fi is that if you're ever out of Verizon's 3G network coverage, you can still get online.

To connect to a Wi-Fi network for the first time, you'll need to turn on the wireless features. Then, you can scan for available wireless networks. Finally, you'll need to be able to read and understand what your wireless network connection indicators offer in the way of information regarding the network you're connected to.

If you're worried about battery life, turn on the wireless capability when you know you are within range of a network you want to access, and turn it off when you know you are not.

Connect Your BlackBerry to Your Wireless Home Network

If you have a wireless network at home, connect to it as detailed here. If the network is faster than what you get from your service provider, you may opt to always connect to the network. If it's slower, you can opt not to.

To connect to your home network:

1. On the BlackBerry menu screen, click Setup.
2. Click Set Up Wi-Fi.
3. Click Next to get started.
4. To locate your home network, click Scan for Networks.
5. Click Turn Wi-Fi on.
6. Click the network to connect to. Figure 10-1 shows an example of what you might see.
7. If prompted for a key, input the key (noting that keys are case-sensitive), and then:
   a. Click Connect or Save. (If you click Save, the network will appear as a profile, and you'll be connected automatically.)
   b. If you clicked Save, verify that the Wi-Fi Network will be saved as a profile.
   c. Rename the network if desired.
   d. Click Next.
8. Click Finish.

Instead of scanning for networks, you can opt to manually add a network. If scanning does offer the network you want, you'll have to go this route. Before starting, locate the notes you took regarding your wireless network name, security type, user name, password, security key, certificate number, and/or other settings; you'll be prompted for this information.

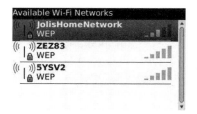

FIGURE 10-1   When you scan for networks, you'll see a list of available networks.

Connect Your BlackBerry to a Public Hotspot and Use the Hotspot Browser

If the wireless features of your phone are enabled, and you know you're in range of a free public hotspot, you can scan for the network and connect. Public places like coffee shops and cafes offer this service to get you to come in and spend money on other amenities, and these places attract users who carry netbooks and laptops. You can enjoy the service too, though, and jump onto the network with your BlackBerry.

1. On the BlackBerry menu screen, click Setup. (Alternatively, you can go to Manage Connections.)
2. Click Set Up Wi-Fi.
3. Click Next to get started, noting that you can opt to hide this screen from now on.
4. Click Scan for Networks.
5. Click the network to connect to, as shown in the following illustration. Most public wireless networks are "open" and thus do not require a password or key.

 Click Save if you want to connect to this network automatically every time you're within range of it.

6. Click Finish.

 Most public hotspots are free and require no registration information. You can perform an Internet search to find the free hotspots in your area. On occasion, though, you may be stuck in a place where you have to pay for Wi-Fi service to use it, or supply registration information. If prompted, click Wi-Fi Hotspot Login to fill out the required information. To return to the Wi-Fi Setup Complete screen, press the Escape key.

When you're at a hotspot, consider switching to the Hotspot browser. This browser differs from the Internet browser you use most of the time, in that it connects directly to the Internet, bypassing servers you usually encounter along the way. With a HotSpot browser, data flows from your phone, to the hotspot, to the Internet, and back. With the "Internet Browser" setting (the default), data flows from your phone to your service provider's servers, to RIM, to BIS, and finally, to the Internet, and then it flows back along the same path. While you may not understand this, all you really need to know is that the HotSpot browser is faster, even if you can't really tell one way or the other. To make this change:

1. On the BlackBerry menu screen, click Options.
2. Click Advanced Options, and then Browser.
3. Change the default browser configuration from Internet Browser to HotSpot browser.

Manage Wireless Networks and Connections

The wireless network profiles you've saved will appear on the Wi-Fi Profile list, and you'll be able to tell what network you're connected to easily (it'll have a green check mark by it). You can change the order of the networks on the list to tell your BlackBerry which wireless networks you prefer over others. When scanning, your BlackBerry will start at the top of the list and work down, attempting to connect to any of these networks (when Wi-Fi is enabled), so you'll want to put the networks you use most often at the top.

To view the status of a network connection:

- From the BlackBerry menu screen, click Options and then Wi-Fi. Figure 10-2 shows this screen.
- From the BlackBerry menu screen, click Setup and Set Up Wi-Fi, and then click Wi-Fi Options.

You'll notice that there are also two settings you can configure:

- **Enable single profile scanning** When this setting is enabled (ticked), your BlackBerry will stay connected to a particular profile when more than one wireless network in the list is within range. This prevents your phone from automatically switching to another saved profile in the same range. When this setting is disabled (unticked), your Wi-Fi connection will be switched, connecting to networks in the order they appear in the profile list, as they become available.
- **Prompt me for manual connection or login** When you are within range of a hotspot that is also a saved Wi-Fi profile and requires a manual login, your device will prompt you to log in. You can disable this by clicking "Don't prompt me again." To enable this feature again, tick this box.

 If a hotspot is open, you'll be connected to it when you're within range, automatically, and with no prompt. You'll also be connected automatically to your home network after you've set it up as a saved profile. In the latter scenario, you will not be prompted again for your security key.

FIGURE 10-2 Here, two Wi-Fi Profiles are saved. One is JolisHomeNetwork and the other is Gold's Gym Garland.

Read Network Connection Indicators

There are a lot of icons, letters, and numbers that can appear at the top of your BlackBerry's screen. Many have to do with your connection.

- **Wi-Fi**   When you see the Wi-Fi icon, Wi-Fi is enabled and you are connected to a wireless network.
- **3G**   The 3G icon tells you you're connected to a 3G network, and you can place and receive calls, send and receive e-mail messages, PIN messages, SMS text messages, and MMS messages, and use the browser to surf the Internet.
- **SOS**   You can only make emergency calls.
- **Off**   Your connection to the wireless network is turned off.
- **X**   You are not in a wireless coverage area.

Manage the Preferred Wi-Fi Network List

Your saved profiles appear under Options, in Wi-Fi. The order of the list is the order in which your phone will search for wireless networks when wireless capabilities are enabled. You want to move your preferred networks to the top of the list, so your BlackBerry does not have to try to connect to networks that you rarely use.

To change the order in which wireless networks appear in the profile list:

1. On the BlackBerry menu screen, click Options.
2. Click Wi-Fi. (If you don't see Wi-Fi, click the Escape key. You may be on a different screen.)
3. Tap the network to move up or down.
4. Click the Menu key and click Move.
5. Tap and then click anywhere in the network list to move the listing there.
6. Click the Menu key and click Save.

Turn Wi-Fi Off

As noted earlier, the constant search for Wi-Fi networks can really drain your battery quickly. Thus, when you are not near a Wi-Fi hotspot and aren't looking for one, turn off Wi-Fi.

To turn off Wi-Fi:

1. Click the Wi-Fi icon on the Home screen, shown in the following illustration. It's at the top of the screen, next to the time and date.
2. Disable Wi-Fi by unticking the Wi-Fi option. You can also disable Bluetooth, or your Mobile network, or turn all connections off.

PART IV

Maps, Media, Syncing, Applications, and Recovery

11

Getting Around with Maps and GPS

HOW TO...

- Turn on GPS
- Get your GPS location
- Get directions to a location
- Get a map from a contact's address
- Locate a restaurant and get directions there
- Watch your own movement on a map
- Send your current location to someone
- Send a map to others
- Create a favorite for a location
- Save a favorite
- Delete a favorite
- Create a favorite for a route
- Make the top of the map always north
- View tracking status
- Clear the map's cache
- Use zoom and pan

Your BlackBerry Storm2 comes with a built-in feature called GPS (Global Positioning System). This means you can have your BlackBerry pinpoint exactly where you are and offer directions to anywhere else. You can also use an application like Google Maps to combine your GPS with Google's map feature to get directions, view images of sites you want to visit, and approximate where you are, should you ever get lost.

GPS can be a tremendous help when you're driving to a new place, looking for a business, or trying to locate a landmark. However (if you're driving or biking), it's important to note that you should either get your directions prior to leaving your present location, or get some kind of cradle for the phone so you don't have to hold and/or look at it while you should be focused on the road.

In this chapter you'll learn about BlackBerry Maps, a free application that offers text-based directions and routes and graphical maps and is included with your BlackBerry Storm2. However, it's important to note that Verizon also offers VZ Navigator for an additional fee, and with it you'll get voice-guided directions along with text and graphics. With voice, you won't have to stop and read the directions; they'll be read to you. VZ Navigator is available from your BlackBerry menu screen, and at the present time, costs approximately $10 a month for use in the United States.

Use BlackBerry Maps

You have more than one option for getting directions from one place to the next. BlackBerry Maps is already installed and ready to use, making it the easiest option. With BlackBerry Maps you simply press Maps on the BlackBerry menu screen and input the appropriate information.

You can also opt for Google Maps, which offers more features than BlackBerry Maps, including satellite pictures, traffic information, and more. Google Maps does not come preinstalled on the BlackBerry Storm2, so if you want it, you'll have to download it.

 To get Google Maps, visit m.google.com/maps and follow the directions for download.

In this chapter we'll focus on BlackBerry Maps (after all, it's a book about the BlackBerry), although after a bit of use you may decide that Google Maps offers more of what you need and opt to give that a try. If you've experienced BlackBerry Maps, you won't find using Google Maps much different.

Turn On GPS

Out of the box, your BlackBerry is only configured to offer GPS information for 911. This means if you call 911 in an emergency, the 911 operator will be able to pinpoint your location without you having to do anything (in theory, anyway). GPS is not enabled for the GPS software on your phone as it could compromise your privacy. So, if you open Maps before enabling GPS, you won't be able to pinpoint your location.

To enable GPS for Maps on your BlackBerry Storm2:

1. On the BlackBerry menu screen, click Options.
2. Click Advanced Options and then click GPS.
3. For GPS Services, choose Location On. See Figure 11-1.
4. Click the Escape key and click Save.

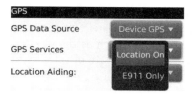

FIGURE 11-1 You have to change the GPS Services option from e911 to Location On if you want to pinpoint your own location.

Get Your GPS Location

You can tell your BlackBerry to identify your current location for the purpose of obtaining your latitude and longitude for a search party or geotagging game, to refresh the location shown from the last time you obtained it, or to see where you are in reference to the world around you. Getting your GPS location is the first step in getting directions, too. You can opt to start from "Where I Am" and forgo typing your actual address. Let your GPS do the work for you!

To obtain your present location:

1. On the BlackBerry menu screen, click Maps.
2. Click the Menu key and click Find Location. See Figure 11-2.
3. In the next screen, click Where I Am.

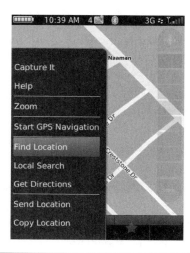

FIGURE 11-2 Pinpoint your own location by clicking Find Location.

It can take a couple of minutes for the phone to find your location, particularly when you're first using the device, since it has to lock on to the GPS satellites and contend with factors such as the weather, buildings, terrain, and so on. All of these things can affect the rate of satellite acquisition.

4. Tap lightly on the right side of the screen to zoom in and out of the map.

Get Directions

You can use your GPS feature to get directions to anywhere, from anywhere. With BlackBerry Maps you can type an exact location to go to or from, a city name for more generic searches, or you can choose to get directions from your current location or anywhere on a map that you have open. No matter what you choose, you can get door-to-door (or city-to-city) directions to (and from) just about anywhere.

To get directions using BlackBerry Maps:

1. From the Maps application, press the Menu key.
2. Click Get Directions.
3. To get directions, make a choice regarding the starting place:
   a. To use your current location, click Where I Am.
   b. If you do not want to use your current address and instead want to identify a new location, type the address in the Enter (or Select) Start Location field. Click Advanced if you need to type a specific address, city, state, zip code, and/or country or if you've been unable to locate what you want on the map using other means.
4. To specify a saved location, click Favorites. You can configure a favorite now for home or work if you like; just click Home or Work under Favorites to get started. (You'll learn more about favorites later in this chapter.)

 To populate your Favorites list, find your location on the map, click the Menu key, and click Add to Favorites.

5. To specify a recently viewed location, click Recent, and click the location.
6. To specify an ending location, enter a destination using one of the methods mentioned in the previous steps.
7. Select Route Preferences, shown in Figure 11-3.
8. Click Search.

 Press the Menu key and click Reverse Directions to get the information in the opposite direction.

9. Click the Menu key and View Directions to view a turn-by-turn list.

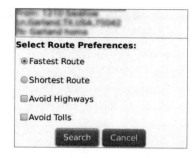

FIGURE 11-3   The Route Preferences settings let you choose the type of route to take.

 The BlackBerry's backlight only stays on for two minutes. If you're driving and have the phone in a cradle, this might hinder your efforts to get to where you're going safely. If this becomes a problem, consider a utility called BBLight. You can search for it online.

Incorporate Contacts

You can get a map to a location from information stored in Contacts. You have to have previously configured an address for a contact, though, so if you need to, input an address for a contact in your Contact list. Once you've accessed the map, consider adding the contact as a favorite for future reference.

To get a map of a contact's address:

1. From the BlackBerry menu screen, click Contacts.
2. Locate the contact and tap the name lightly to select it.
3. Click the Menu key and click View < *Work or Home* > Map.
4. Map opens with the location, where you can then get directions as detailed earlier. See Figure 11-4.
5. To make the location a favorite, so that you can open it from inside the Maps application the next time you need it, click the Menu key and click Add to Favorites.
   a. To navigate to the location using your current location as a starting point, click the Menu key and click Navigate to Here. Zoom in or out to see the bigger (or smaller) picture of the route.

FIGURE 11-4   You can have Maps open from Contacts.

Locate a Restaurant (or Business) and Get Directions There

You search for and view specific locations on maps. For instance, you may want to view businesses close to you, or specific points of interest like airports, landmarks, schools, or parks. You may also want to find something near your location, like a specific restaurant, hotel, or club, or you can search for more generic terms like coffee, gas, or bank. Here, we'll search for Applebee's, a local restaurant, and get directions to it from our current location.

To obtain directions to a specific location near you using BlackBerry Maps:

1. In a map, preferably a map that denotes your current location, press the Menu key and click Local Search.

 To quickly get your current location, click the Menu key and click Find Location. Then, click Where I Am.

2. Type the location you'd like to find, perhaps the name of a restaurant. Click Enter on the keyboard.
3. Browse the results and select one.
4. Click View On Map to see all of the instances of the restaurant chain. See Figure 11-5.
5. Use the Zoom features to locate the business. Click it to view the address.
6. Click the Escape button to return to the list; select the instance of the business you want, if more than one exists.

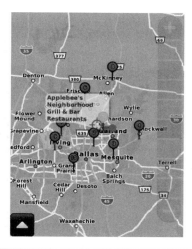

FIGURE 11-5 To view the establishment or point of interest on a map, click View On Map.

7. Click the Menu key, and click Navigate To Here, Call (if a number is provided), Copy Details, or any other option that suits you. If you click Navigate To Here, a map will be provided from your current location to the new one.
8. Click the Menu key and click View Directions for a turn-by-turn list.

Watch Your Own Movement on a Map

You can track your own movement on a map when you're in motion. This is a great feature to enable when you're riding a train or bus, taking a road trip, or perhaps even lost in a big city or the woods! By watching and following your own movements, you can tell easily what direction you're heading, where you're heading to, and approximately how fast you're getting there. As with GPS, GPS navigation is not enabled by default, due to privacy issues that could arise.

To watch your own movement on a map, you have to enable the feature:

1. On the BlackBerry menu screen, click Maps.
2. If necessary, click the Escape key. Then, press the Menu key and click Find Location. Click Where I Am.
3. Click the Menu key again, and click Start GPS Navigation. (Sometimes this is referred to as GPS tracking.)
4. As you move, a small dot will move on the screen denoting where you are.
5. To stop GPS tracking, press the Menu key and click Stop GPS Navigation.

Remember that a GPS connection can be interrupted by several factors. If you don't have a clear view of the sky or if you go into a tunnel or underground subway, for instance, your Storm2 may lose your location temporarily.

Get Your Current Location and Send It to Someone

You can send your location via text, e-mail, PIN, and more. First, you have to locate your position with the Where I Am command, and then you can send your position to anyone at all. You should spend a few minutes learning how to send your current location, just in case the need ever arises because you're lost, in an accident, trapped, or simply trying to communicate how far you are from your destination.

To send directions or your location:

1. On a map, obtain your current location. (Click the Menu key, click Find Location, click Where I Am.)
2. Click the Menu key and click Send Location.
3. Choose the message type: E-mail, PIN, MMS, Messenger Contact, and others.
4. Complete the message by adding a sender, typing a message, and then click Send.

 The recipient of your location message will receive a link that contains map data including longitude and latitude. They will have to click the link to see where you are, using an Internet connection.

Share and Save GPS Data

GPS isn't just about you and your location. Often, you'll get directions for someone else or you'll want to share the directions you've found for the purpose of meeting someone at an agreed-upon location. In these cases, you'll want to send the map to other people. You may also decide to save a map (including directions for getting there) for future reference, should you need to visit the same place again or forward the information to someone else the next time you go there. This is called *bookmarking* a location or a route, and it's how you populate your Favorites list.

You can also save locations, like the address of your business or your home. When you save a location, you can use it as a start or end point any time you get directions to or from there. It really simplifies the process surrounding obtaining directions.

Send the Map to Others

You can send directions (a route) you've acquired to someone you know via e-mail, text, or other method. To send directions, first, use BlackBerry Maps to obtain the directions and the desired route. Then, press the Menu key to see your sending options.

To send a route to someone else:

1. In Maps, get directions from a location to a location. If you're sending the map to a friend, consider creating a Start location close to where you know they are.

Tip When getting directions for a friend, choose From Map in the Start Location page. Scroll through the map to locate a major intersection for their reference.

2. With the route mapped, click the Menu key and click Send Directions. See Figure 11-6. Your recipient will receive turn-by-turn directions and a link to a graphical map.
3. Choose how to send the map: E-mail, PIN, MMS, and so on.
4. Type the name of the person you want to send the map to, type a message, and send the message.

Create and Manage Favorites

You can do a lot with location favorites and GPS. You can create favorites for your most visited places so you can create a route, get and share directions, or find a location quickly. You can delete a favorite you no longer need easily, so it's okay to create a favorite every time you map a location, just in case.

To create a bookmark for a location:

1. Map the location to mark as a favorite using any method detailed in this chapter.
2. Press the Menu key and click Add or Favorites.
3. If you like, click next to Label to change the title.
4. Click OK.

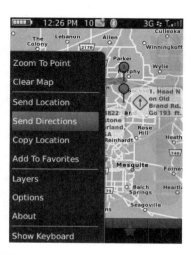

FIGURE 11-6 When viewing a map, click the Menu key and click Send Directions.

To delete a bookmark for a location or route:

1. In the Maps application, click the Menu key.
2. Click Find Location.
3. Click Favorites and highlight the favorite to delete.
4. Press the Menu key again and click Delete.
5. Click Yes to confirm.

To create a favorite for a route:

- In Maps, get directions to a location. To get a route, click Navigate To Here when it's an option.
- With the map showing on the screen, click the Menu key.
- Click Add to Favorites.
- If you want, change the name; click OK.

Personalize GPS

You can personalize how GPS looks and acts when you're using it. You may want to always have the map point north, for instance, or zoom in or out of a map to better navigate it. You can configure other settings too, like viewing your tracking status at the bottom of a map (or not). You can even clear the map's cache to erase the data you've acquired.

Make the Top of the Map Always North

When you're walking or driving with your BlackBerry and incorporating GPS into it, you may be happy with the configuration of the map. The top of the map shows which way you're moving when GPS tracking is on, by default. With this being the case, the top of the map doesn't always point north. Sometimes you want to view the map with the top of the map always pointing north. This will allow you to give better directions by simply looking at the phone, without having to perform any calculations regarding the direction.

To configure the map to always point north:

1. On a map, press the Menu key.
2. Click North Up.

Note   Track Up and North Up are a toggle. North Up always shows the screen with North facing up. Track Up shows the screen in the direction you're moving.

View Tracking Status

If you use BlackBerry Maps and track your status with GPS tracking, you can opt to view tracking status or not view it. Tracking status shows your speed and information about the satellites you're accessing, and it is sometimes necessary. However, tracking status, when shown on the Dashboard, takes up part of the screen you might rather have for the map. In this case, you'll want to hide it.

With GPS tracking on, you can show or hide the tracking status at the bottom of the screen, called the Dashboard. To hide the Dashboard (and show it again):

1. In a map, press the Menu key and click Options.
2. Click Hide Dashboard. (Alternately, click Show Dashboard.)

Clear the Map Cache

The map cache keeps information regarding past searches, directions, and routes you've taken. You may want to clear the cache to protect your privacy, or to keep information secret regarding where you've been.

To clear the map cache:

1. While in any map, press the Menu key.
2. Click Options.
3. Press the Menu key again (although it may seem counterintuitive to do so).
4. Click Clear Cache. See Figure 11-7.
5. Click Delete.

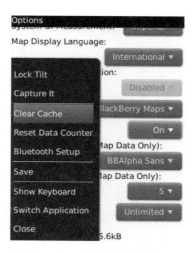

FIGURE 11-7   Clear the Cache to erase information you've acquired in Maps.

Zoom Options

There are a few zoom options that are available from the Menu options. You can Zoom To Point, for instance, to immediately zoom in on your start or end points; you can use your finger to zoom in and out; and you can even access zoom from the Menu options.

While you're in a map, try these zoom features:

- Click the Menu key and click Zoom to Point.
- Click the Menu key and click Zoom.
- Click inside a map to zoom in; click the minus sign on the screen to zoom out.

 To pan a map, slide your finger in any direction.

12

Tether Your BlackBerry to Your Computer

HOW TO...

- Meet system requirements
- Install the Desktop Manager Software
- Download and install the VZAccess Manager
- Connect your BlackBerry to your PC
- Connect to the Internet
- Troubleshoot connectivity problems

Your BlackBerry Storm2 can serve as an external modem for your laptop or personal computer. This is called *tethering*. Once the connection is made, you can access the Internet from the computer through the BlackBerry's cellular connection. Tethering is ideal when you need to connect to the Internet from your laptop but don't have access to a free Wi-Fi hotspot or a public or private network, or if you don't have an always-on Internet connection for the computer.

 In this chapter I'll assume you purchased a phone from a retailer and it was not "unlocked," that you use Verizon, and that you are willing to pay for the right to tether your device and are not trying to use your BlackBerry in any manner that is in violation of your contract with your provider.

Did You Know? **Stay Away from Tethering Hacks**

You may be tempted to try one of the many techniques available to tether your phone for free, by hacking the "standard modem" settings on your PC, using initialization commands, and dialing out to the Internet through your connected BlackBerry. Although it may be possible to tether first and ask questions later, it's best to give Verizon a call ahead of time and do it the legal way. Your contract with Verizon does not allow you to tether your phone without informing them and paying an additional fee. Just because it's possible doesn't mean it's legal.

Meet System Requirements

In order to tether your phone, you'll first need to contact your provider (Verizon, in the United States) and tell them so. You'll have to sign up for additional services (and pay more), because tethering requires additional bandwidth. At the time this book was written, you could get 5MB (megabytes) of data usage for $30 a month with a qualifying plan. Five megabytes equals approximately 5,000KB (kilobytes). That's quite a bit of data, and is enough for most people, but you should check your usage a couple of times a month to make sure you're not going over, just in case. (There's more on how to do this later in this chapter.)

You will also need to perform the following tasks and meet the following requirements:

- Verify that the PC you'll use has an operating system of Windows 2000 or higher or, if your system is Mac, that it has 10.4 or higher.
- Install the BlackBerry Desktop Software; this includes the BlackBerry drivers you'll need to use your phone as a modem.
- Download and install the VZAccess Manager on your PC.
- Connect a USB cable from your phone to your PC and connect the BlackBerry.
- Install any updates to the software on the computer and/or the phone itself.
- Watch your Internet usage.

Install the Required Software

A PC uses some form of a modem for connecting to the Internet. You can use an old-fashioned dial-up modem, a cable modem, or a DSL modem. Of course, you can have Wi-Fi connection too, and the hardware you need for that is sometimes referred to as a Wi-Fi modem. Your computer will look to a modem to connect to the Internet, one way or the other. In order to use your BlackBerry for Internet access, then, you need to make your computer think the *phone* is a modem. Only then can you get connected through it.

Configuration tasks involved in tethering cell phones have previously been quite complex. You used to have to configure the modem settings first, add a few commands, and then you had to configure "dialing options" for the new "modem" you added. The dialing options you configured would actually trick your PC into thinking it's using a real modem to dial a number for Internet access.

Today, it's much easier. You only need to install specific software, which includes the Desktop Manager software that came with your phone and the VZAccess Manager available from the Internet. Once both of those are installed, connecting is easy.

Install the Desktop Manager Software

The CD that came with your BlackBerry contains the drivers and software required to tether your phone to your computer. You have to install that CD first.

To install the Desktop Manager Software:

1. Open the CD/DVD drive door and insert the CD.
2. If you are prompted to run the program, click Run. If you aren't prompted, click the CD icon in the Computer window and click Start, and then click Run.
3. Select your language and click Begin.
4. There are several options on the CD including User Guide, Learn to Type with SureType, and Safety and Product Information. Click the option for BlackBerry Desktop Software.
5. Click Install BlackBerry Desktop Software.
6. Click Next to get started, and then choose your language and click Next again.
7. Click "I accept the terms in the license agreement" and click Next.
8. Choose who can use this program (only you or anyone who accesses the computer) and click Next.
9. Choose Typical for the setup type. Click Next.
10. Choose to install or not to install any additional programs (like BlackBerry Media Sync or Roxio Media Manager), and click Next.
11. Choose the type of e-mail account you'll integrate (or have already integrated), and click Next.
12. Choose the startup options, including Start BlackBerry Desktop Manager Automatically When the Computer Starts, Create a Shortcut for BlackBerry Desktop Manager on the Desktop, and Check for Software Updates. Click Install.
13. Click Finish.

 If you need to install the software on a netbook that does not have a CD drive, you can either share a drive on a networked computer and access the CD from there, or download the program from the Internet. Visit www.blackberry.com and search for Download Desktop Manager software.

Download and Install the VZAccess Manager

The VZAccess Manager is the second program that must be installed onto your computer. This program is not included on the BlackBerry User Tools CD that came with your phone, though, so you'll have to connect your computer to the Internet using a method that does not yet involve your BlackBerry, download and install the program, and then configure it.

On your PC, locate and download VZAccess Manager:

1. Connect to the Internet via your home network, work network, or public hotspot.
2. Navigate to www.vzam.net/BlackBerry.
3. On the left side of the page, click VZAM Software, as shown in the following illustration.

BlackBerry® Software Updates

4. Choose your operating system under What Operating System Are You Using?
5. Choose PDA/Advanced Device under What Device Are You Using?
6. Choose BlackBerry PDA under What Hardware Are You Using?
7. Enter your wireless number and click Continue.
8. Click Download Now.
9. Click Run.

Once the software has finished downloading and you've clicked Run to start the installation, complete the installation:

1. Click Next to start the installation process.
2. Click "I accept the terms in the license agreement" and click Next.
3. Verify that Install Desktop Shortcut is ticked and click Next.

Did You Know? **Install as Often as You Want**

You can install both the Desktop Manager Software and the VZAccess software on as many computers as you like and tether your phone to them as well. Just be mindful of how much data you're using.

4. Verify that the installation folder is where you'd like the program to install (it's best to leave this as it is) and click Next.
5. Choose Typical for the setup type and click Next.
6. Click Install.
7. Click Finish.

Before continuing, reboot your computer. Start the BlackBerry Desktop Manager and connect your phone. Install any updates before continuing here.

Make the Connection

Once all of the software is installed, you are ready to tether your BlackBerry and connect to the Internet through it. You'll need to locate your USB cable, the one that came with your phone, before continuing. You'll also need to start the programs in a particular order to avoid any problems. So before starting, reboot your PC, start the BlackBerry Desktop Manager, connect your phone, and then start the VZAccess Manager.

To connect your BlackBerry to your PC and connect to the Internet through it:

1. Make the physical connection using the USB cable that came with your phone.
2. Wait while any drivers are installed. If prompted to install updates, do so.
3. Double-click the shortcut to the VZAccess Manager on your Desktop.
4. If you are within range of a wireless network and your computer is configured to connect automatically, it will connect and you'll see the connection in the VZAccess Manager window, shown in Figure 12-1.

If you can connect to a home or work network or hot spot, do so. Those networks generally offer unlimited data usage while tethering does not.

5. If no other connection is available, double-click Verizon Wireless – VZAccess. (It may be the only connection option you see.)
6. When you're prompted that this Mobile Broadband connection is not free, and that charges will apply, click Continue. Note that you can opt not to show this message again.
7. You will see that you're connected in the VZManager window. Note the option to disconnect from the WWAN.
8. Click the Internet icon on the Taskbar to navigate to any web page.

When you're finished with the Internet, click Disconnect WWAN at the bottom of the VZAccess Manager window.

There's one last, very important thing. You should check your current data usage statistics often to make sure you don't exceed your data limit. You can check your usage from the My Verizon icon on your BlackBerry menu screen (or from the My Verizon web site using any computer).

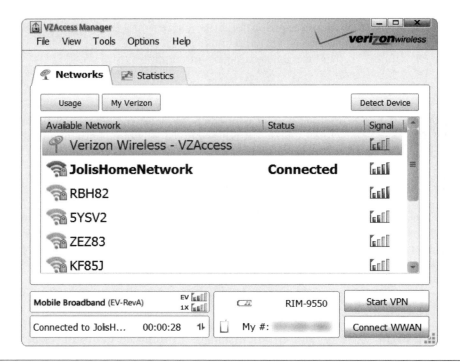

FIGURE 12-1 The VZAccess Manager window shows the VZAccess option as well as other wireless networks in the area.

Troubleshoot Connectivity Problems

If you've been following along and performed all the steps in this chapter, double-clicked the Verizon Wireless – VZAccess option in the VZAccess Manager window, but could not get connected, you'll have to do a bit of troubleshooting. Unless your screen shows you're connected, you aren't.

If you're having problems connecting first, reboot your PC. Start the Desktop Manager Software, connect your BlackBerry, and try the VZAccess Manager again. Most of the time this works to resolve problems.

 If you've previously tried to configure your PC for free tethering, the changes you made to the Standard Modem and other configurations are likely the source of your problems now. If that's the case, consider a System Restore on any Windows PC to remove the changes you made.

If you still can't get connected, make sure your computer recognizes the BlackBerry. In the VZAccess Manager window, click Detect Device, and then click Start. Wait while your phone is detected. This will resolve the problem if detection

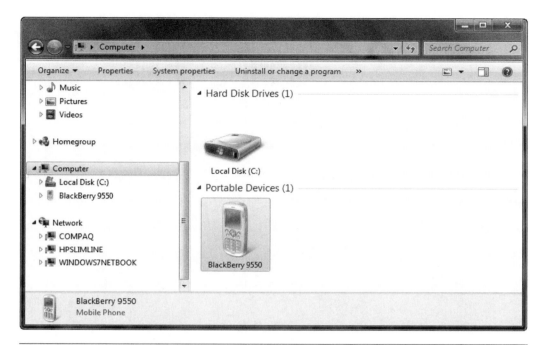

FIGURE 12-2   When your PC is connected, you should be able to see your BlackBerry in the Computer window of any PC.

was unsuccessful. If you receive an error that the device was still not detected, verify that the cable is securely connected to both the phone and the computer. Additionally, verify that the USB port you're using works, by plugging in another device to test it. If you can't see your BlackBerry, neither can your computer! See Figure 12-2.

 Click Start and click Computer on a PC to view your device.

If you still can't get connected, you may have to call Verizon and ask for assistance. Dial *611. They are there to help you. If you purchased an "unlocked" phone and are using it with a different provider, you will probably not get the help you need with a phone call, though, and will have to search the Internet for assistance.

Finally, if nothing works, complete the steps again on another PC, preferably a laptop. If it works on one PC but not another, at least you've found out that the problem is not with your cable, and may lie in the PC's hardware or modem configuration. If problems persist, take the laptop, power cord, phone, and USB cable to your local Verizon store. Happy tethering!

13

Get Music on Your BlackBerry

HOW TO...

- Install and launch Media Manager
- Drag a file from your computer to your BlackBerry
- Move multiple files from your computer to your BlackBerry
- Sync music
- Sync photos

You can copy music, photos, videos, and other data from your computer to your BlackBerry and then access the media (and data) anytime you like, wherever you are. You have several options for transferring media from your computer or laptop, including using BlackBerry Media Manager and BlackBerry Media Sync. Both are included on the User Tools CD that came with your phone, and they are also available for download from the web. If you installed the User Tools CD earlier, you probably have both programs on your computer already.

You can also purchase music from various online stores from your computer or right from your phone. Verizon has teamed up with Rhapsody to provide access to millions of songs from thousands of artists, for a monthly fee. You can access songs from your computer, transfer music to your phone, or purchase music from the online store, directly from your phone. The V CAST Music | Rhapsody option is available from the Application Center on the BlackBerry's menu screen. You use that application as you would any other; you install, subscribe, and then work through the directions given to use the program.

In this chapter, you'll learn how to copy (transfer) the music, photos, and other media you already have on your computer to your BlackBerry using the two programs included on the User Tools CD: Media Manager and Media Sync. Both are accessible from the Desktop Manager Software after installation. If you decide after using these two programs that you'd like to subscribe to a music-sharing site like Rhapsody, you can explore those options later.

If you already belong to a music subscription service on your computer, there may be no need to also subscribe to Rhapsody. You can easily manage music on your computer and connect the phone when applicable to sync it.

Use BlackBerry Media Manager

BlackBerry Media Manager is part of the Desktop Manager Software. Hopefully, you've already installed this CD, but if you haven't, do so now. With Media Manager you can access the songs, pictures, videos, and other multimedia files that are already on your computer and transfer them to your phone. You can also copy files from your phone to your computer using the same interface. The latter is a good way to get pictures off your phone and onto your computer. Whatever the case, using Media Manager is a manual job, and you are in charge of what gets moved, when, and where it is to be stored. You can even define the quality of music you copy, where Media Manager should look for files, and more.

Install and Launch Media Manager

Media Manager may not yet be fully installed on your computer. To install it, you have to connect your BlackBerry to it, start the Desktop Manager Software, and then:

1. On your computer, from the Desktop Manager Software window, click Media.
2. Click Install under Media Manager. (If it says Launch, it's already installed.)
3. Once the software has been installed, click Launch.
4. Once the software has launched, click "I accept the terms in the license agreement" and click OK.
5. You may see various pop-ups; if so, simply close them, but make a note that one of those pop-ups allows you to view the files on your BlackBerry phone from your computer. This offers another way to transfer data (using a drag-and-drop technique), and is often more efficient than using either of the applications introduced in this chapter.

 You'll need to use Media Manager on a computer or laptop with a resolution of 1024 by 768 or higher. Media Manager won't start if this condition isn't met.

Drag a File from Your Computer to Your BlackBerry

After installing and launching Media Manager, you'll see a split screen on the Media Manager interface. The top screen represents the media on your computer; the bottom screen represents the media on your BlackBerry. You can navigate the top part of the screen to locate songs and media that are on your computer. You navigate the bottom part of the screen to locate media folders on your BlackBerry.

When both parts of the Media Manager interface are configured such that you can see media (such as a song or album) you'd like to copy from your computer to your BlackBerry (or vice versa), you can drag the files from one screen to another to perform the copy operation:

1. Connect your BlackBerry to your computer using a USB cable.
2. Drill down to locate media (such as a song, video, or photo) to copy from your computer to your BlackBerry, using the top pane of the Media Manager window.
3. Drill down to locate the appropriate folder on your BlackBerry where you'd like to store the copied data.
4. Drag the file from the top pane to the bottom one.
5. Wait while the file is copied and if prompted, choose Convert for Optimal Playback, if you like. You can also opt for no conversion or advanced conversion options.
6. Wait while the data copies. See Figure 13-1.

Media Manager isn't just for managing music; you can also perform copy tasks with photos and videos, too. However, Media Manager can seem slow and limiting if you're used to the navigational options in Windows Vista, Windows 7, or Macs, and you may opt for a different method for transferring files.

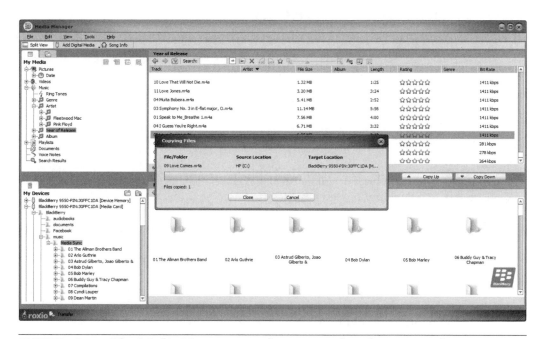

FIGURE 13-1   The Media Manager interface is complex, showing a split screen to separate the files on your computer and the files on your BlackBerry.

You may have noticed the option to Copy Up or Copy Down while inside the Media Manager. Instead of dragging, you can select the media you want to copy in either partition, and select one of these to copy the data up or down (to or from either device).

Move Multiple Files from Your Computer to Your BlackBerry

You can copy more than one piece of media at a time when transferring data to and from your computer and BlackBerry. You can also drag the data or simply click Copy Up or Copy Down to complete the copying tasks. To select more than one song at a time:

- When selecting music (or other data), hold down the Shift key to select contiguous songs (or videos or pictures).
- When selecting music (or other data), hold down the Ctrl key to select noncontiguous songs (or videos or pictures).

When copying to your BlackBerry, make sure you're copying to the Memory Card and not to Device Memory. Both are available in the bottom partition.

Use BlackBerry Media Sync

BlackBerry Media Sync is the second option from BlackBerry Desktop Software (under Media) for media management, and may already be installed on your computer. If it is not, simply click the Install button under BlackBerry Media Sync (in the Desktop Manager Software window) to install it. As the name implies, BlackBerry Media Sync allows you to configure syncing between your phone and your computer. Once the software has been installed, click Launch. If you see a notice that an update is available, install it before continuing.

When you click Launch, you may see various pop-ups from your computer's operating system; ignore them and close them after noting what they offer (such as the ability to view the files stored on your BlackBerry).

The first time you open Media Sync you'll be prompted to configure it. You can:

- Name your device (or change the name of it, actually)
- Choose where to save media on your phone (choose Media Card)
- Configure the amount of space to keep free on your memory card (the default is 10 percent)
- Set your preferred music library (iTunes or Windows Media Player)

Sync Music

Once you're inside the BlackBerry Media Sync application, you'll see two tabs: Music and Pictures. Choose the Music tab to choose what music you want to sync with your phone. Figure 13-2 shows an example of an iTunes music library, selected tracks and playlists, and a visual representation of how much space the media will require from the phone's memory card. Select the items to sync and click Sync Music.

 After syncing is complete, you may find that Media Sync could not sync all of the songs you selected. This is likely caused by trying to copy protected content. You can view the songs that would not sync after the process completes.

Sync Photos

As with syncing music, you can sync pictures with BlackBerry Media Sync. It's not a sophisticated program, though; the only good working option is to copy the entire Pictures folder on your computer to the Pictures folder on your BlackBerry. It's likely

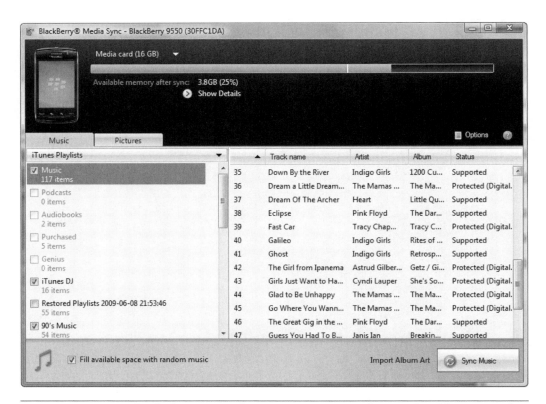

FIGURE 13-2   With BlackBerry Media Sync, you can configure what libraries and playlists you want to sync, even if it's iTunes.

you won't want every picture transferred, though, so this poses a problem. Media Sync won't let you browse subfolders in your Pictures folder either (if you've created them), and pictures are all lumped together in one window. While there are better options for getting pictures on your BlackBerry from your computer, for the sake of completeness I'll show you how to use Media Sync here. (I'll include a Did You Know Box for copying pictures using the Computer window.)

To copy pictures from your computer to your BlackBerry using Media Sync:

1. Open the Desktop Manager Software on your computer.
2. Click Media.
3. Launch BlackBerry Media Sync.
4. Click the Pictures tab.
5. Click the Pictures folder in the left pane and tic it to sync all photos.
6. Click Sync Pictures.

Did You Know?

Drag and Drop for Easy Data Management

When you connect your BlackBerry to your computer, you'll see an icon for it in the Computer window. You may also see a pop-up that allows you to "Open folder to view files." In fact, you may see two of each of these things (one for the phone itself and one for the media card inserted into the phone). Drill down into the Folder icon for the media card to find the Pictures folder on it. Once you're there, you can easily drag and drop data from your computer, including entire folders, subfolders, or one piece of data at a time.

14

Search for, Play, and Manage Media Files

HOW TO...

- Play a song
- View a picture
- View a video
- Listen to a list of music and shuffle the songs
- Create a new playlist and add songs to it
- Play a playlist
- Shuffle songs in a playlist
- Move songs around in a playlist
- Record your voice and play it back
- Send a voice note via e-mail or MMS
- Access and manage ring tones

If you worked through Chapter 13, you have music on your BlackBerry Storm2. If you've followed along in the book from the beginning, you have ring tones, pictures, and videos, too. Now you're ready to listen to your music, create and play playlists, view pictures and videos, and see what else you can explore that's media-related.

 Most of this chapter is about music, because other types of media have already been covered in this book.

Play, View, and Manage Media

The Media button on the BlackBerry menu screen is your key to unlocking all things media! That's where you'll find access to the subfolders Music, Videos, Pictures, Ring Tones, Voice Notes, Video Camera, and Voice Notes Recorder. In this chapter, you'll explore just about all of these, and remember, if you decide you want to access any of these subfolders more easily, you can always move them to your BlackBerry menu screen.

Play a Song, View a Photo, View a Video

Let's start out with the basics, playing a single song, viewing a single photo, or playing a single video. While doing that, you can also explore three of the Media subfolders to familiarize yourself with them.

To play a song:

1. On the BlackBerry menu screen, click Media.
2. In the Media folder, click Music.
3. Select any folder. You may see the following:
   a. Go to V Cast Music | Rhapsody
   b. All Songs
   c. Artists
   d. Albums
   e. Genres
   f. Playlists
   g. Shuffle Songs
4. Depending on your selection in Step 3, continue to drill down to locate the music to play. Figure 14-1 shows the Artists list, with an artist highlighted. Once you've located the song to play, click it.
5. Use the volume buttons on the outside of the phone to raise or lower the volume.
6. Use the controls at the bottom of the screen to restart the song from the beginning, pause the song, stop the song, or to play the next song in the folder.

 Tip   Plug in headphones or ear buds if you can't hear the music or do not want to disturb others around you.

To view a picture:

1. On the BlackBerry menu screen, click Media.
2. In the Media folder, click Pictures.
3. Select any folder. You may see the following:
   a. All Pictures
   b. Picture Folders
   c. Sample Pictures

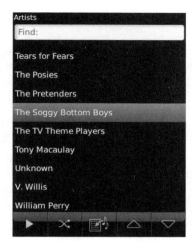

FIGURE 14-1   Drill down into any folder or subfolder to find the desired song.

4. Depending on your selection in Step 3, continue to drill down to locate the picture to view.
5. Click any picture once to view it in full-screen mode.

The default for picture management is "thumbnail view," which allows you to view small thumbnails of images prior to clicking to view them. However, you can opt for "list view" to see a list of names instead.

To view a video:

1. On the BlackBerry menu screen, click Media.
2. In the Media folder, click Videos.
3. Click any video once to view it in full-screen mode. (Playing a video automatically switches the screen orientation from portrait to landscape mode.)

Listen to a List of Music and Shuffle the Songs

You can listen to a specific list of music, say the music from a particular album, and, if you like, shuffle the songs when they play (so they play in random order). You can also listen to songs by a single artist, and shuffle those as well if desired, so that you can focus on one artist and nothing else. In fact, any music that's in a list, whether the tracks are sorted by artist, genre, album, or other method, can be played and/or shuffled.

To listen to a specific list of songs and/or shuffle those songs during playback:

1. On the BlackBerry menu screen, click Media.
2. In the Media folder, click Music.
3. Select any folder. Choose one of the following:
   a. All Songs
   b. Artists
   c. Genres
4. Depending on your selection in Step 3, continue to drill down to locate the music to play. For instance, in the Genres list, you can opt for Classical, Folk, Jazz, Rock, and others, and then choose All once you're in the desired category. Depending on how much music you have, you may have to drill down further. However, once you're into a list of songs, you're ready for Step 5. See Figure 14-2.
5. Once you've found the folder containing the songs to play:
   a. Click the Play button to play all the songs in the folder starting with the one you selected, in the listed order.
   b. Click the Shuffle button (the right button with two crossing arrows right below the track progress bar) to play all the songs in the folder in random order. It won't matter what song is highlighted when you click Shuffle; the phone will decide which song plays first.
6. Use the volume buttons on the outside of the phone to raise or lower the volume.
7. Use the controls at the bottom of the screen to restart the song from the beginning, pause the song, stop the song, or to play the next song in the folder. You can even repeat a song!

FIGURE 14-2 You'll need to get to a folder of songs to play them. Select any song in a folder and click Play or Shuffle, as you like.

Work with Playlists

A playlist is a list of songs you select, give an appropriate name to (like Party Songs, Quiet Time Music, Exercise, or Coffee Break), and play whenever you're in the mood for that particular list of songs. You can create playlists on your phone or your PC. If you previously created playlists on your computer, and then transferred songs and playlists from your computer to your phone as detailed in Chapter 13, you already have playlists on your phone. If you've never worked with playlists, you can create one on your phone easily. Once playlists are available, as shown in Figure 14-3, you simply select them to play them.

Create a New Playlist and Add Songs to It

It really doesn't matter if you already have a playlist or not, or transferred a playlist from your computer; what you'll do here is create a new playlist from the songs on your phone. First, though, put some thought into what kind of playlist you'd like. You may want to create a group of songs for exercising, for relaxing, or for hanging out with friends.

 Music isn't just for iPods any more. There are several manufacturers who offer external speaker systems, "juke boxes," and music amplifiers built just for your BlackBerry. With them, you can share the music on your phone with anyone in the vicinity.

To create a new playlist on your BlackBerry:

1. On the BlackBerry menu screen, click Media.
2. Click Music.
3. Locate the first song you'd like to add to your new playlist. Tap it to select it. (If you click it, the song will play.)

FIGURE 14-3   You may already have playlists on your phone if you transferred playlists you created on your computer to your phone as detailed in Chapter 13. Here, there are five playlists already available.

4. Click the Add to Playlist button as shown in the following illustration.

5. Because you're creating a new playlist, click New Playlist.
6. Type a name for the playlist.
7. Click OK.
8. Repeat Steps 3 and 4 for each song you'd like to add. After clicking Add to Playlist, select the new playlist you created in Step 6. My new playlist is named "My favorite songs," as shown in Figure 14-4.

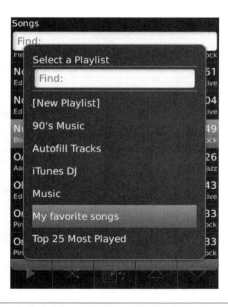

FIGURE 14-4 After you click Add to Playlist, all playlists appear as well as the option to create a new playlist. To add music to an existing playlist, click the playlist name.

Add Multiple Songs at Once

You can add entire lists of music to a playlist. For instance, you can drill down into Artists, tap an artist's name, and then click Add to Playlist. This will add all of that artist's songs to the playlist. The same is true of albums and genres. (You can't add playlists to other playlists, though.)

Play a Playlist

After creating a playlist, it's easy to play it. You simply select it from the Playlists list. You can also play any playlist while also shuffling the songs in it during playback. You can move songs around in a playlist too, which may be useful if you're using the list to play songs in a specific order; for example, a playlist for exercise: slow songs for warm-ups and cool-downs, and faster songs for the more intense portions of your workout.

To play a playlist:

1. On the BlackBerry menu screen, click Media.
2. Click Music.
3. Click Playlists.
4. Click the desired playlist and click the Play button to start playback.

To shuffle songs in a playlist during playback:

1. On the BlackBerry menu screen, click Media.
2. Click Music.
3. Click Playlists.
4. Tap the desired playlist.
5. Click the Shuffle Songs button.

To move songs around in a playlist:

1. On the BlackBerry menu screen, click Media.
2. Click Music.
3. Click Playlists.
4. Click the desired playlist.
5. Highlight any song, and then click the Move button (the middle button at the bottom of the screen).
6. Use your thumb or finger to drag the selected song up or down positions in the playlist.
7. Click to apply the change.
8. Click the Escape key and click Save when finished.

Explore Other Media

While you were inside the Media folder, you probably noticed a few things you may not have explored, including Ring Tones, Voice Notes, and Voice Notes Recorder. All three applications are quite easy to use and likely don't need much direction, but for the sake of completeness, I'll include a few notes about them here.

Record Your Voice and Play It Back

The Voice Notes Recorder lets you record personal notes to yourself or others, or to record something going on around you (like your snoring spouse). Once you've recorded a note, you can save it, play it back, delete it, or even share it with others. To get started, record your own note.

To record a voice note, play it back, and then send it via e-mail or SMS:

1. On the BlackBerry menu screen, click Media.
2. Click Voice Notes Recorder.
3. Click the Record button and start talking. Press the button again when you're finished. (Note that the recording is now paused, which means you can click the Record button again to continue, if desired.)
4. When you've completed your recording, note the options (shown in Figure 14-5) and select one:
   - **Continue recording** To continue recording where you left off.
   - **Stop** To stop recording and save the note to the Voice Notes folder.
   - **Play** To play back the recording.

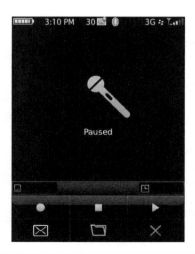

FIGURE 14-5 After you've recorded a note, you'll see several options including the option to rename or delete.

- **Send**   To send the note via MMS or e-mail, or to an instant messaging contact.
- **Rename**   To rename the note to something more applicable, like Grocery List or To Do List.
- **Delete**   To delete the note and not save it.

 There's no Save option because all voice notes are saved automatically with their default name to the Voice Notes folder under Media.

5. Click Play to hear your note.
6. Click Send to send the note. Complete the message by adding a recipient and clicking the Send button.

 You can delete unwanted voice notes or otherwise manage them after the fact from the Voice Notes folder under Media. Just select the note and click the Menu button to see your options.

Access and Manage Ring Tones

Finally, there's the Ring Tones folder. Here you can manage any ring tones you've purchased, the ring tones that came with your BlackBerry Storm2, and easily set any tone as your default ring tone.

To play or set any ring tone or to delete a ring tone you've purchased:

1. On the BlackBerry menu screen, click Media.
2. Click Ring Tones.
3. Click All Ring Tones to access every ring tone on your phone; click My Ring Tones to access only the ring tones you've purchased.
4. Click any ring tone to play it.
5. To apply a ring tone:
   a. Tap it to select it.
   b. Click the Menu key.
   c. Click Set as Ring Tone.
6. To delete any ring tone you've purchased:
   a. Click My Ring Tones.
   b. Tap the ring tone to select it.
   c. Click the Menu key.
   d. Click Delete.

15

Use the Calendar and the Clock

HOW TO...

- Access the Calendar
- Choose a view
- Create an appointment
- Send an appointment using MMS
- View a specific calendar
- Change default calendar settings
- Create a reminder
- Configure sound options for reminders
- Set/answer an alarm

Your BlackBerry Storm2 comes with several features to help you manage your time. There's the Calendar for keeping track of appointments and activities and a clock to help you keep track of the time. The clock also features an alarm you can use to remind you of commitments, wake you up in the morning, and even let you snooze, should you need a few more minutes to compose yourself. You can even keep a calendar synchronized with a third-party application, like Microsoft Outlook.

Use the Calendar Application

The Calendar is available from the BlackBerry menu screen and opens in "Day" view the first time you use it, and later, in the last view applied. In the Day view, you can easily access today's appointments and your agenda, among other things. You can also toggle among views for day, week, or month, using a button on the screen, or see the next or previous day's agenda with a single click. While you're in the Calendar, from the Menu button you can opt to set new alarms, go to a specific date, or quickly move to the previous day, next day, previous week, or next week. It all starts when you access the Calendar and explore the Calendar interface.

Access the Calendar

You can access the Calendar from the BlackBerry menu screen, and once it's open, you can view its features. Open the Calendar and locate the following on the bottom of the screen:

- The Calendar window. Click anywhere in the window to create a new entry or appointment.
- The New button in the bottom-left corner. Click here to create a new appointment.
- The View button. Click here to toggle views from Day, to Week, to Month. You can create a new appointment in any view. Figure 15-1 shows Month view.
- The Today button (in the middle). Click it to quickly return to today's view.
- The Previous button:
  - When in Day view, click this button to see the previous day's calendar.
  - When in Week view, click this button to see the previous week's calendar.
  - When in Month view, click this button to see last month's calendar.
- The Next button:
  - When in Day view, click this button to see the next day's calendar.
  - When in Week view, click this button to see the next week's calendar.
  - When in Month view, click this button to see next month's calendar.

You can also click the Menu button from any Calendar view to access various options, including but not limited to:

- **Go to Date**   To go to a specific date by scrolling through calendar days and dates.
- **Previous**   To go to the previous day, week, or month, depending on the view.
- **Next**   To go to the next day, week, or month, depending on the view.

FIGURE 15-1   You can view the Calendar by day, week, or month.

- **New Alarm**   To set a new alarm with a subject, time, date, and recurrence, as applicable.
- **New**   To create a new appointment with a start and end date, reminder, recurrence, and the option to make the appointment private.
- **View Agenda**   To view a list of appointments, meetings, and other events in a list.

Choose a View

In any Calendar window, you can easily change the view by clicking the View button at the bottom of the screen. Note the Calendar icon at the bottom of the window. It's the second from the left, next to the New icon (and before the Today icon). Press it to see what view you'd be in if you clicked the icon. Figure 15-2 shows Week view, but clicking the icon would offer Day view. In any view, the Previous and Next buttons allow you to navigate quickly to another day, week, or month.

Create an Appointment

If you use the Calendar regularly, you'll need to know how to create appointments. Appointments appear on the Calendar and can be configured with a subject, location, and start and end times. You can even choose a specific e-mail or third-party application to send your appointment to others if you want to share the information. If you choose to share the appointment, you may also opt to configure a time zone, change your status to Tentative, Busy, Out of Office, or Free; mark it as a conference call; set a recurrence; or mark it private. You do all of this from a single window.

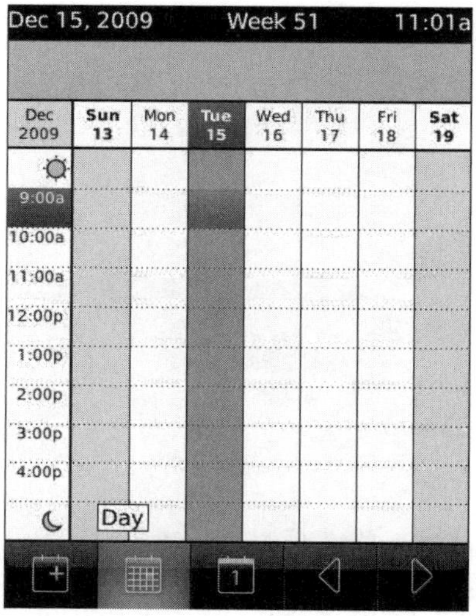

FIGURE 15-2   Click the Calendar icon at the bottom of the screen to switch views.

It's important to note that a calendar is created for each e-mail account you configure on your BlackBerry. Calendars are also created for third-party applications you use, like Facebook. All appointments appear on the default calendar, but if you opt to save appointments to multiple calendars, you can view each calendar separately. You'll learn how to view appointments applied to a specific calendar shortly. For now, when you create an appointment, be mindful of the type of appointment it is, and what calendar it should be applied to, should you ever want to separate say, your work appointments from your personal ones.

To create a new appointment:

1. Access the New Appointment window in one of the following ways:
   a. In Day view, click the time and day inside the window that represents when you'd like to set the appointment.
   b. In Week view, click the day of the week and the time of day you'd like to set the appointment.
   c. In Month view, click the day to set the appointment, and then in that day's window, click the time the appointment should start.
   d. In any view, click the Menu button and click New.
2. Choose a Calendar under Send Using:
   a. To save your appointment to a specific calendar, choose the calendar's related e-mail address.
   b. If you plan to send the appointment using MMS, select the account you'd like to send from if more than one exists. In Figure 15-3, Hotmail is selected.
   c. For work-related appointments, choose your work e-mail and related calendar.
   d. For personal appointments, choose your personal e-mail and calendar.
   e. For appointments that have to do with a third-party application, like Facebook, select the appropriate entry. Note that at the present time, sending an appointment via MMS to Facebook only results in the subject line being published.
3. Although you do not have to input any information to save the appointment, consider inputting a subject and a location.

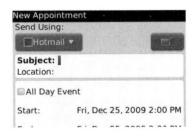

FIGURE 15-3   If you want to send the appointment using MMS, choose the account to send from. Then begin creating your appointment by typing a subject and location.

4. Configure other options applicable for the appointment, including if it's a recurring appointment.
5. Click the Save button at the top of the page. It looks like a folder. Alternately, click the Menu key and click Save.

After creating an appointment, select it. At the bottom of the window, locate the Invite Attendees icon. Click this icon to invite others to join you at the appointment (which may now be referred to as a meeting).

Send an Appointment Using MMS

You may opt to create an appointment and send that appointment via MMS, for the purpose of sharing it with others. If you send a calendar appointment to a device or application that recognizes the file format (.vcs), the person on the receiving end will be able to open and view the appointment. If you send the appointment to a device or application that does not recognize the file format, the recipient will only get the subject of the message. The following illustration shows how the message will appear to a recipient who receives the appointment on a PC running Microsoft Office Outlook 2007. The recipient only need click the attachment (titled Test.vcs) to open and view it.

If a recipient receives your appointment on a device capable of reading .vcs files, they'll be able to open and view your appointment, and even incorporate it into their own calendars.

Phones and applications that will recognize this file format include but are not limited to:

- BlackBerry phones that include calendaring features
- Apple iCal
- Microsoft Entourage
- Microsoft Outlook
- Microsoft Works Calendar
- Various PDA software programs including Palm Desktop

To send an appointment using MMS to anyone or any device:

1. In any Calendar view, tap the appointment to send.
2. Click the Menu key and click Send As MMS.
3. Select a recipient from the Contacts list.
4. If more than one entry is available for that contact, select the desired entry.
5. Complete the message and click the Mail icon to send it.

FIGURE 15-4 You may have several options for saving and sending a calendar appointment.

View a Specific Calendar

By default, a calendar is created each time you create an e-mail account and when you install and use applications like Facebook. All appointments, no matter what calendar they are saved to, appear in the default Calendar view. You can opt to view a specific calendar, though, to see only the entries related to that particular calendar. (You apply a specific calendar to an appointment when you create it.) Figure 15-4 shows four options during appointment creation. If you have similar calendar options, here's how you may opt to use them:

- **Facebook**   For anything related to Facebook contacts, including get-togethers, happy hours, birthdays, and the like.
- **Hotmail**   For family appointments only, including dinners, birthdays, doctor's appointments, and games.
- **BlackBerry**   For work-related appointments only, and for appointments sent by other BlackBerry users.
- **Time Warner**   For personal appointments that are configured as "Private."

To choose a specific calendar to only view entries related to that calendar:

1. From the BlackBerry menu screen, click Calendar.
2. Click the Menu button.
3. Click Select Calendar.
4. Click the Calendar to view.

Change Default Calendar Settings

The Calendar assumes many things about you that may not be true. For instance, it assumes you work from 9 A.M. to 5 P.M. It assumes the first day of your week is Sunday. It assumes that, when you click Snooze, you want 5 more minutes (you may want 15). You can change these defaults and others from the General Calendar Options page.

To change the default calendar settings:

1. In any Calendar view, click the Menu key.
2. Click Options.
3. Click General Options.
4. Make changes as desired, including things like Confirm Delete, Keep Appointments for 60 Days, and how long to snooze.
5. Click the Escape key and click Save.

Configure Reminders and Alarms

A clock and calendar go hand in hand. You need a calendar to manage your months, weeks, and days, and you need a clock to manage your hours. Luckily, your BlackBerry Storm2 has both. You can use these features to create reminders, configure sounds for reminders, and to set and answer an alarm.

Create a Reminder

If you need to remind yourself to do something, create an appointment and a reminder. You may want to set a reminder to stop at the grocery store after work, and have the reminder sound 15 minutes before you're due to get off for the day. You may want to set a reminder to sound two hours before a date, so you'll have time to get dressed, get directions, and get prepared.

To create a reminder:

1. In the Calendar application, create a new appointment using any method detailed earlier.
2. Fill in any information applicable, noting that in the Notes section you can write your grocery list or leave instructions for yourself regarding the reminder.
3. Next to Reminder, click to select an option. Click 2 Hours to be reminded of the event two hours prior to its scheduled start time. See Figure 15-5. Fifteen minutes is the default.
4. At the designated time configured in the reminder, your phone will emit a short, quiet "ding-ding." You can change the sound options though, if you need something a little more intrusive.

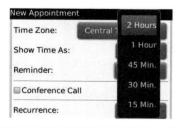

FIGURE 15-5   Set your reminder enough ahead of the appointment that you'll have enough time to prepare but not so much time that you'll forget.

Configure Sound Options for the Calendar and Reminders

If the short, quiet ding that's applied to reminders isn't enough to rouse you to action, you can change it. One way is from inside the Calendar using the Menu button's options. Simply click the Menu button and click Reminder Alerts. From there you can change:

- **Ring Tone**   The default ring tone for the BlackBerry Calendar is BBRelaxed_ Melodious. It's not very loud, and it is easy to miss. If you like, select a new ring tone from the list. Click Try It to hear it.
- **Volume**   Change the volume to something you know you can hear. Your options range from 1 to 10.
- **Count**   The reminder will only ding once. You can change that so that it repeats up to three times.
- **LED**   Choose between On or Off. LED emits a light along with the sound when turned on.
- **Vibration**   Choose from On, Off, or Custom. Click Custom to apply the length, count, and other vibration settings.
- **Notify Me During Calls**   Choose Yes or No to be alerted (or not) while in a call.
- **Try It**   Click Try It to hear your changes.

Set/Answer an Alarm

You set alarms from the Clock or from inside the Calendar. Many people prefer creating alarms from the Clock over the Calendar. You can quickly access the Clock by clicking the time on the Home screen, or by clicking the Clock option on the BlackBerry menu screen. When the Clock appears, click it to view the options:

- **Set Time**   Click to set the current time.
- **Set Alarm**   Click to set an alarm.
- **Enter Bedside Mode**   Click to enter Bedside Mode and prevent the BlackBerry from disrupting your sleep. By default, it will disable LED alerts and dim the screen, but you can change this and other Clock-related options (while you're in the Clock application) by clicking the Menu key and clicking Options.
- **Stopwatch**   Click to start the Stopwatch application.
- **Timer**   Click to start the Timer application.

    To set an alarm:

1. On the BlackBerry menu screen, click Clock.
2. Press the clock's face and click Set Alarm.
3. Use the wheel to set the clock and turn it on.

More Ways to Access What You Need

You can access New Alarm from inside the Calendar application. Just press the Menu key.

It is possible to sync various calendars you keep on your computer. For example, if you have your Outlook e-mail configured to sync to your BlackBerry, your BlackBerry will automatically pull in your Outlook appointments and sync them. However, some calendars, like iCal, require desktop software like BlackBerry Desktop Software for Mac to perform syncing tasks.

16

Explore Applications

HOW TO...

- View available applications
- Write a memo
- Create a task
- Use the calculator
- Download MySpace (or Flickr)
- Explore MySpace (or Flickr)
- Explore Password Keeper
- View files
- View saved messages
- Get To Go updates
- Use Word To Go
- Explore Sheet To Go
- Use Slideshow To Go
- Learn keyboard shortcuts

Your BlackBerry Storm2 comes with quite a few applications, including those that allow you to create task lists, type memos, perform calculations, save passwords, and even post information and data to Flickr and MySpace. It also offers a few file-related applications, such as Word To Go, Sheet To Go, and Slideshow To Go, that enable you to work with and share data while away from your computer. Such data include Word documents, spreadsheets, and presentations, for starters. Of course, with the ability to access files such as these, you'll also need a way to manage them, by using the Files icon in the Applications folder.

In this chapter, feel free to review the available applications in the first section, and then skip to the part of the chapter that contains the information for the applications you're interested in. If you want to create task lists, skip to the "Create a Task" section. Likewise, if you want to review a Microsoft Office PowerPoint presentation on your phone, refer to the section "Use Slideshow To Go."

Understand and Use Applications

The applications we'll discuss in this chapter are all located in the Applications folder on the BlackBerry Menu screen, but as with other applications you use often, you can move these out of this folder and onto the BlackBerry Menu screen if you prefer. These applications can help you be more productive, share data more easily, stay organized, and keep your data more secure. The first step to using these applications is to access them. Once you know where they are, you can begin using them to round out your BlackBerry experience.

To view available applications:

1. On the BlackBerry Menu screen, locate Applications.
2. Click Applications to open the Applications folder.
3. View the available applications. See Figure 16-1.

Write a Memo

One of the easiest applications to use is MemoPad. Memos are notes you write to yourself or others for the purpose of remembering something later. Think of a memo as a Post-It note you can share. After writing the memo, you can e-mail it to someone else, post it to Facebook, or attach it to an instant message.

1. In the Applications folder, click MemoPad.
2. Click the Add Memo option at the top of the MemoPad screen.

FIGURE 16-1 There are plenty of applications to explore.

3. Type a title.
4. Click inside the writing area and type your memo.
5. Click the Save icon.
6. Note the new memo in the memo list. See Figure 16-2.
7. Note the icons at the bottom of the interface. They are
    a. Edit
    b. Forward As
    c. Delete
    d. Scroll Up
    e. Scroll Down
8. With any memo selected, click the Forward As icon.
9. Select how to forward the message. You may see an option like Facebook or Messenger Contact, but you will certainly see:
    a. Email
    b. PIN
    c. SMS Text
    d. MMS
10. Select the desired option and complete the forwarding memo.

Create a Task

Sometimes you need to do more than write a memo; you need to create a task. A task is a chore or an assignment that you will either complete or pass on to someone else to complete. As with memos, you can save tasks in the Tasks list, and then e-mail them, post them to a web page, or forward them to a messaging contact. By forwarding a task, you pass the task on to that person. Remember that a task is a job someone needs to complete (versus a memo, which is simply a reminder or a note).

FIGURE 16-2 Memos are saved in a memo list that appears each time you click the MemoPad icon in the Applications folder.

Because a task is a job, when creating a task you have access to more features than memos. For instance, when you create a task you can include the following information, none of which is available in a memo:

- **Task**   Type a task name.
- **Status**   Choose from Not Started, In Progress, Completed, Waiting, and Deferred.
- **Priority**   Choose from High, Normal, or Low.
- **Due**   Choose from None or By Date. Choosing the latter allows you to set a deadline for completing the task.
- **Time Zone**   Choose any time zone you want.
- **Reminder**   Choose from By Date or Relative. Relative brings up options for ranging from 0 minutes to one week.
- **Recurrence**   Choose from None, Daily, Weekly, Monthly, or Yearly.
- **Categories**   Choose a category (Business or Personal). Clicking the Category field doesn't bring up this option, though; to apply a category, you'll have to click the Menu button and then Categories.
- **Notes**   Type list notes.

 Set a yearly recurrence task for your anniversary, important birthdays, and similar items.

Once you've created a task, it appears in the Tasks list. The options on the screen include Mark Completed, Mark in Progress, Delete, and Scroll Up and Scroll Down. However, with a task selected (highlighted), you can click the Menu key to access more options. Forward As is one of them. When you forward the task, essentially you are passing it on to someone else. If that's what you want to do, make sure to include a message that says so; otherwise, the person on the receiving end may not fully understand that the task is for them to complete!

To create a task (and forward it to someone else):

1. On the BlackBerry Menu screen, click Applications.
2. In the Applications window, click Tasks.
3. Click Add Task.
4. Type a name for the task.
5. Select the desired setting for the task. See Figure 16-3.
6. Type notes for the task.
7. In the top-right corner, click the Save icon.
8. Back at the Add Task pane (which appears automatically after you've saved a task), note the icons at the bottom of the screen. This is where you'll mark the task complete or in progress, or delete the task later.
9. Click the Menu key, and click Forward As.
10. Choose how to forward the task—Email, PIN, SMS Text, MMS, or other option.
11. Complete the forwarding process by selecting or inputting a contact, adding a note, and providing other information as warranted.

FIGURE 16-3   There are plenty of settings to choose from. (The keyboard is hidden so you can see the options.)

If you think you may forget about the task, create a reminder or e-mail the task to yourself. Most people access their Inbox often, and having a reminder there can be helpful.

Use the Calculator

The calculator is another application in the Applications folder. While it allows you to do things you'd expect, like add, subtract, multiply, and divide, it also offers a memory option, the option to input negative numbers, to get the square root of a number, and to change a number to a percent. You can also get the reciprocal of a number, should you ever need to.

Now all of that is just great, but wait, there's more! It's a conversion calculator too. You can convert a number that's in miles to kilometers, gallons to liters, and inches to centimeters, and back again, to name a few.

To use the calculator and to convert data to and from metric:

1. From the BlackBerry Menu screen, click Applications.
2. Click Calculator.
3. Type in any number and experiment with the basic features including add, subtract, multiply, divide, square root, and percent.
4. With any number input, click the Menu button.
5. Click To Metric.
6. Click In -> Cm.
7. Click the Menu key again.
8. Click From Metric.
9. Click Cm -> In.
10. Repeat until you are comfortable with the calculator.

Explore MySpace and Flickr

If you use Flickr and/or MySpace on your computer at home, you can incorporate your user account with your BlackBerry. Flickr is a photo and video sharing web site, complete with an online community platform. With Flickr, you can easily share photos and videos with whomever you like. There are places to post comments and manage your data too. MySpace is a social networking site, like Facebook, where you can upload photos, blog, keep a personal profile, create groups, and have similar social networking fun. If you're already part of one or both of these sites and would like to extend it to your BlackBerry, read on. If you'd like to explore these sites to see if they're right for you, well, that's best achieved at a desktop computer.

To download MySpace (and Flickr is similar):

1. From the BlackBerry Menu screen, click Applications.
2. Click MySpace (or Flickr, if you prefer).

 These instructions are for MySpace, but using Flickr is similar.

3. Click Download.
4. Select your language and click Next.
5. Click Set Application Permissions, and then click Download.
6. Review the list of permissions. The defaults are probably fine, but review them anyway. Once you're finished, click the Escape button. The download process will begin.
7. Click OK once the installation has completed.
8. If you're prompted again to choose a download language, click the Escape key twice. This seems to be a bug in the BlackBerry download process.
9. Click the Applications folder again, and again, click MySpace.
10. Scroll through the disclaimer and terms of use, and click I Agree.
11. Log in with your account information, click Save My Password if you wish, and click Login.

Explore MySpace (and Flickr is similar):

1. In the Applications window, click MySpace (or Flickr).
2. Input your user account information.

 You'll See New Send/Share Options!

From now on, when you want to share a photo or video, you'll have more options than the usual MMS and e-mail. You'll now have Send to MySpace or Send to Flickr! This makes it easy to upload photos to your new space.

FIGURE 16-4   Once you're logged in to MySpace, you'll see icons at the top of the page.

3. Note the icons at the top of the page, shown in Figure 16-4.
4. Click each icon to view the data in it. Try Mail, Friend Updates, Comments, and My Photos. Note that in My Photos, you can upload a photo and view your photo albums, as shown in Figure 16-4. This is a good way to get started.

Explore Password Keeper

The Password Keeper application is very useful if you have a lot of passwords to keep track of. With Password Keeper, you only need to keep track of one password, the one you input in the Password Keeper. The application does the rest.

The data Password Keeper stores is kept in the Application Memory on the BlackBerry Storm2. It is not stored on the microSD card, which makes it more secure. The only way to transfer the data from Password Keeper on your phone to another BlackBerry device is to create a backup and to use the BlackBerry Desktop Manager on your computer.

With Password Keeper, you can store passwords for:

- Search engines
- Bank accounts
- Web sites
- Facebook, Flickr, MySpace
- Internet shopping sites
- Travel sites
- Investment sites
- And more

 If you input an incorrect password into the Password Keeper ten times in a row, all of the stored passwords will be erased from your BlackBerry Storm2.

To set up and use the Password Keeper:

1. From the BlackBerry Menu screen, click Applications.
2. Click Password Keeper.
3. Type a password and type it again to confirm.
4. Click OK.
5. To add a password for a web site, click the Menu key and click New.
6. Type a title, username, password, and web site. Include notes if you like.
7. Click the Menu button again and click Save.
8. The next time you go to that web site and can't remember your password, input the password you created for Password Keeper to find it there.

Work with Files

You have some files on your BlackBerry Storm2, even if you don't know it. You may have an iTunes Library file, App World files, user files, and more. The only files you need to be concerned with, though, are files you've created and/or saved yourself. These include but are not limited to Word documents, presentations, pictures, videos, and spreadsheets. Files are available for management from a virtual filing cabinet available from the Applications folder.

View Files

To view your files, you'll locate them in the Application folders under Files. Once you've located your files, you can then open them and edit them with one of the "To Go" applications detailed later in this chapter. You can easily see the file properties, and even send the file via e-mail.

 A file's properties include the file name, type, location, size, and when it was last modified.

To view the files on your BlackBerry Storm2:

1. From the BlackBerry Menu screen, click Applications.
2. Click Files.
3. You should see All Documents and My Files (if you don't, click the Escape key).
4. Click All Documents.
5. Note the documents. If you see any you recognize, such as a file ending in .doc or docx (a Microsoft Word document), .ppt or pptx (a Microsoft PowerPoint file), or xxls or xlsx (a Microsoft Excel file), note that those files can be opened and edited with the "To Go" applications detailed later in this chapter.
6. Click the Escape key to return to the previous screen.

FIGURE 16-5   Drill down to view what's in the Documents folder.

7. Drill down through the folders as follows to locate the Documents folder, shown in Figure 16-5:
   a. Click My Files.
   b. Click Media Card.
   c. Click BlackBerry.
   d. Click Documents.
8. Remember this location in the "Use To Go Applications" section; you'll browse here to locate a file to view and edit.

Available Folders

Most of the folders you'll be working with in the Files application are under the location spelled out in this section: My Files\Media Card\BlackBerry. You'll see lots of folders including but not limited to:

- Audiobooks
- Documents
- Music
- Pictures
- Podcasts
- Ringtones
- Videos
- Voicenotes

And you may see folders for applications you've installed, like Facebook. Browse these folders now to see what is in each one. You can delete any item you recognize by clicking the Menu button and then Delete. This is one way to free up space on your media card and keep it free of unwanted data.

View Saved Messages

You may have noticed another icon a few spots over from Files in the Applications folder, Saved Messages. This folder holds messages you've saved in the Messages folder on the BlackBerry Home screen. Even if you delete the original message in the Messages folder, a copy of the message (because it was saved) will still be available here. This way you can keep your Inbox clean and organized while storing messages you want to keep in their own space.

 To save a message in the Messages folder, click the Menu button and click Save.

To view your saved messages and manage them:

1. On the BlackBerry Menu screen, click Applications.
2. Click Saved Messages.
3. Scroll through the saved messages.
4. For any message, note that you can open or delete it. If you open the message you can then reply to the message, forward the message, or delete the message.

Use To Go Applications

Your BlackBerry Storm2 comes with DataViz's Documents To Go Suite, which includes three applications: Word To Go, Sheet To Go, and Slideshow To Go. You get the Standard Edition of Documents To Go for free, but you can upgrade to the Premium Edition if you need more functionality. The Standard Edition lets you work with Microsoft Word, PowerPoint, and Excel files, and view, edit, and save them, among other things.

 The version of your To Go applications may need to be updated. When the BlackBerry Storm2 shipped, the version number for the To Go apps was 1.008, and now Version 2.001 is available. See the next section, "Get To Go Updates," for more information.

The following list details the features of the Standard To Go applications:

- Microsoft Word, Excel & PowerPoint for Windows (97, 2000, 2003, and 2007) support
- Microsoft Word, Excel & PowerPoint for Macintosh (98, 2001, 2004, and 2008) support
- Open e-mail attachments
- Open side-loaded documents (via media card and BlackBerry Desktop Manager)
- BlackBerry shortcuts support
- BlackBerry hardware features (trackball, scroll wheel, QWERTY) support
- SureType/Multitap support
- Rich file viewing (text and cell formatting, graphics, tables, zoom, alignment, bullets and numbers, and so on)
- Basic file editing (edit and select text, cut/copy/paste, undo/redo, and so forth)

As noted, Premium applications exist, but you'll have to purchase them. The Premium applications do much, much more, including offering Adobe PDF support, creating new files, inserting hyperlinks into documents, and more. To see what features you can expect from the Premium applications, in any To Go application, click the Menu key and click Try Premium Features.

Get To Go Updates

First things first; you need to see if an update is available for your Documents To Go applications and install it.

1. From the BlackBerry Menu screen, click Applications.
2. Click Word To Go.
3. Click the Menu button and click Check for Updates.
4. Click Yes to connect to the Internet.
5. If prompted that a free update is available, click Download Now to install it.
6. If prompted to register, do so. (Make sure to opt out of their mailing lists, unless you want to receive updates on their products.)
7. Once you're registered, click the appropriate option to download the update.
8. Click Download, and click Yes to continue.
9. Reboot the phone when prompted.
10. The first time you start Word To Go or any other To Go application, you'll have to accept the terms of service and opt to Use Standard to follow along here, as shown in Figure 16-6.

 Before you continue, at your personal computer, send an e-mail to your BlackBerry phone that contains a Word document, an Excel file, and a PowerPoint file.

FIGURE 16-6   Once you've updated Documents To Go, you'll need to tell the application you'd like to use the Standard edition.

Use Word To Go

You can do quite a bit with the Standard edition of Word To Go. You can perform basic editing; save files; e-mail files; cut, copy, and paste data; and apply basic font formatting, for starters. You can also use a Find function, among other things. Before you can do any of this, though, you have to have a Word file to work with. E-mail yourself a Word file from your computer, or have a friend e-mail you one before you continue.

1. Locate a Word file. You may have one as an attachment in an e-mail or in the Files folder discussed earlier.

 You can open Word To Go and click Open a File if you prefer.

2. Click the file to open it, and click Open Attachment if necessary for an e-mail.
3. When prompted, click Edit with Documents To Go, shown partially in Figure 16-7.
4. Click the Menu key, and click Edit Mode. If you see View Mode, you're already in Edit Mode. It's a toggle.
5. To select data to ultimately copy, cut, or paste, or send via e-mail:
   a. Click the Menu button and click Select. (Note that Select All is an option.)
   b. Drag your finger on the page to select the desired data. You can also try touching the start and end points with two fingers.
   c. Click the Menu button again to view Cut and Copy options, to cancel the selection, and to send via e-mail.
6. To apply formatting to text:
   a. Select the text as detailed earlier.
   b. Click the Menu button and click Format.
   c. Choose the type of formatting to apply: Bold, Italic, or Underline. See Figure 16-8.

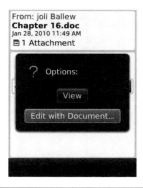

FIGURE 16-7 Click Edit with Documents To Go when opening a Word file.

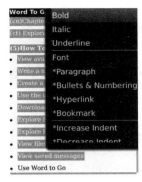

FIGURE 16-8   The Menu button offers several options, but the ones with asterisks beside them are only available in the Premium versions.

   Any item that has an asterisk (*) beside it is not available in the Standard edition, only the Premium edition. If you click it, you'll be prompted to purchase or try out that version.

7. To locate a word:
   a. Click the Menu button, and click Find.
   b. Input the text to find, select Case Sensitive or Words Only if you wish, and click Find.

Explore Sheet To Go

You can do quite a bit with the Standard edition of Sheet To Go. You can navigate Excel files, view cell contents, change zoom levels, find and replace data, and perform basic editing, like clearing cells; using cut, copy, and paste; working in rows and columns; and more. Before you can do any of this, though, you have to have an Excel file to work with. E-mail yourself an Excel file from your computer, or have a friend e-mail you one before you continue.

To open an Excel file so you can explore the Sheet To Go interface:

1. Locate an Excel file. You may have one as an attachment in an e-mail or in the Files folder discussed earlier.

   You can open Excel To Go and click Open a File if you prefer.

2. Click the file to open it, and click Open Attachment if necessary for an e-mail.
3. When prompted, click Edit with Sheet To Go.
4. Click the Menu key, and click Edit Mode. If you see View Mode, you're already in Edit Mode. It's a toggle.

Keyboard Shortcuts

When in View mode, you can use keyboard shortcuts to navigate your Word document, Excel file, or PowerPoint presentation.

Here are a few things to explore in Sheet To Go:

- Click the Menu button and click Go to see navigation options.
- Click the Menu button and click Worksheets to show another sheet in the file.
- Select any cell to edit what's in the cell, or to cut, copy, select, or save the data in it.
- Click the Menu button and click Select, and then drag your finger across the screen to select data on it. See Figure 16-9.
- Click the Menu button and click Zoom to access the zoom options.
- Click the Menu button and click Find to access the Find and Replace options.
- Click the Menu button and click Row (or Column) to select, insert, or delete these items.
- Click any cell and click Edit cell to edit its data.
- Click any cell, and then click the Menu button. Click Function to view the functions you have access to and can input.

 Most advanced Excel features aren't available in Standard; you'll have to get Premium to gain access to options like inserting sheets, formatting numbers, using AutoSum, and inserting a new cell comment.

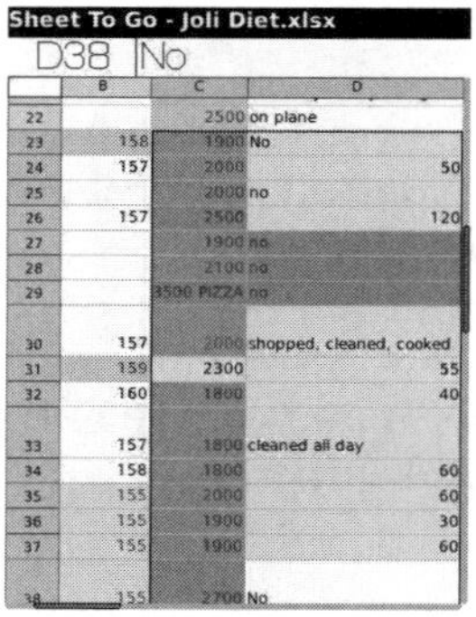

FIGURE 16-9   Select data to cut or copy the data, clear the cells, e-mail the data, delete it, or to perform other tasks.

Use Slideshow To Go

You can do quite a bit with the Standard edition of Slideshow To Go. You can navigate the slides in a PowerPoint presentation, zoom in and out, edit slide text and bullets, select text to cut, copy, e-mail, and the like, and more. Before you can do any of this, though, you have to have a PowerPoint file to work with. E-mail yourself a PowerPoint file from your computer, or have a friend e-mail you one before you continue.

1. Locate a PowerPoint file. You may have one as an attachment in an e-mail or in the Files folder discussed earlier.

 You can open Slideshow To Go and click Open a File if you prefer.

2. Click the file to open it, and click Open Attachment if necessary for an e-mail.
3. When prompted, click Edit with Sheet To Go.
4. Click the Menu key, and click Edit Mode. If you see View Mode, you're already in Edit Mode. It's a toggle.
5. Notice that the presentation opens on the first slide of the presentation. Note that it can take some time for the entire presentation to load.

 If you get a message that a file can't be opened because a dialog box is open in a Documents To Go application, open each Documents To Go application and close any open dialog boxes or files.

Try the following inside your presentation:

- Use your finger to scroll right to the next few slides, and scroll left again to return to the first slide.
- Click the Menu button and click Zoom to view zoom options.
- Click the Menu button and click Edit Slide Text to edit text on the selected slide. Place the cursor on the screen and edit text as desired. See Figure 16-10.
- Click the Menu button and click Slide Sorter to rearrange the order or the slides. Click the slide to move, and from the resulting dialog box, click Move Up or Move Down.
- Click the Menu button and Delete to delete the slide currently showing.
- Click the Menu button and click Outline to see the presentation in Outline view.

FIGURE 16-10   There are several options from the Menu button, including Edit Slide Text.

TABLE 16-1 Keyboard Shortcuts To Go

QWERTY	SureType	Action
ENTER	ENTER	Scroll down or activate an object.
SPACE	SPACE	Scroll down one page.
SHIFT + SPACE	SHIFT + SPACE	Scroll up one page.
T	1	Jump to the top of the document.
B	7	Jump to the bottom of the document.
N	3	Scroll up one page at a time.
P	9	Scroll down one page at a time.
F	Q	Open the Find dialog box.
Z	Z	Open the Zoom options.

Learn Keyboard Shortcuts

When you're in View mode in any of the Documents To Go applications, you can employ keyboard shortcuts. Table 16-1 shows these.

For more keyboard shortcuts, visit http://www.dataviz.com to locate the Documents To Go User's Guide for your BlackBerry Storm2 model. That document contains keyboard shortcuts for each of the three applications installed on your phone.

17

Verizon Service and Applications

HOW TO...

- Learn about additional services
- Locate available services on the Internet
- Download and install VZ Navigator or VZ Navigator Global
- Start VZ Navigator
- Find a route with VZ Navigator
- Do more with VZ Navigator
- Get started with ringback tones
- Browse ringback tones and purchase one
- Assign a ringback tone to a contact
- Download and install V CAST Music
- Download a song with V CAST Music

The BlackBerry Storm2 is, at the current time, exclusive to Verizon. That means that you pay Verizon each month for service. This is always the case when you purchase a new phone from a Verizon store or authorized reseller, because the BlackBerry Storm2 you'll purchase here will always be "locked," meaning that you must use Verizon for your service provider. However, it is possible to purchase an "unlocked" phone from a third party (not Verizon). If you do this, you can use your BlackBerry Storm2 with another provider, such as AT&T. If you have an unlocked phone and use it with another provider, it's highly unlikely that you'll be able to use the Verizon applications and services detailed in this chapter. Note that unlocking a phone is, of course, frowned upon by Verizon, but other companies generally don't ask questions when you apply for service with them.

In this chapter, I'll assume you purchased a phone from a retailer or authorized reseller, that Verizon is your service provider, and that you are signed up with an unlimited data plan. If all of that is the case, you have access to the Verizon applications and services outlined in this chapter.

Learn About Available Services

There are no shortages of additional services. Some you may be familiar with, like Roadside Assistance and instant messaging, but others may have escaped your notice, including VZ Navigator, ringback tones, and V CAST Music. These applications and services cost extra, and are added to your bill in addition to services you've already signed up for, including your data plan, voice plan, visual voice mail, and other add-ons. If you have extra money to spend and think you may be interested in spending it, this chapter is for you!

The best way to discover the additional services available to you (and the ones you're already signed up for) is to visit Verizon's web site from a desktop computer. You'll want to create a user name and password and sign in, so that you will have a personalized experience at the site. Once you're logged in, click Add/Change Features under Quick Links. You may see something similar to what's shown in Figure 17-1. Here, you can see which services are currently enabled and which can be added.

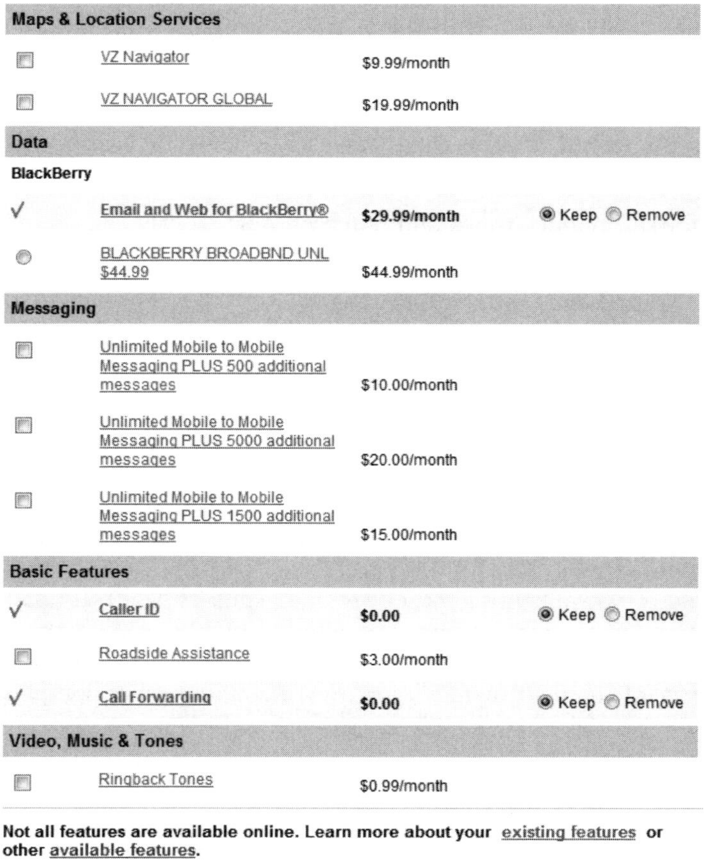

Maps & Location Services		
☐ VZ Navigator	$9.99/month	
☐ VZ NAVIGATOR GLOBAL	$19.99/month	
Data		
BlackBerry		
✓ **Email and Web for BlackBerry®**	**$29.99/month**	◉ Keep ○ Remove
○ BLACKBERRY BROADBND UNL $44.99	$44.99/month	
Messaging		
☐ Unlimited Mobile to Mobile Messaging PLUS 500 additional messages	$10.00/month	
☐ Unlimited Mobile to Mobile Messaging PLUS 5000 additional messages	$20.00/month	
☐ Unlimited Mobile to Mobile Messaging PLUS 1500 additional messages	$15.00/month	
Basic Features		
✓ **Caller ID**	**$0.00**	◉ Keep ○ Remove
☐ Roadside Assistance	$3.00/month	
✓ **Call Forwarding**	**$0.00**	◉ Keep ○ Remove
Video, Music & Tones		
☐ Ringback Tones	$0.99/month	

Not all features are available online. Learn more about your existing features **or other** available features**.**

FIGURE 17-1   Create a user name and password to view your current services and sign up for additional ones.

You can click any entry to learn more about it, but it's best to click the *available features* link shown at the bottom of the page (see Figure 17-1). Click any service from this linked page to enter the support pages to learn more about it. Once in the support pages, you'll have access to even more options, including V CAST Music.

Here are the three services you'll learn about in this chapter:

- **VZ Navigator and VZ Navigator Global**   A GPS mapping and routing system with voice-prompted turn-by-turn directions, with auto-rerouting if you miss a turn. Local searches of over 14 million points of interest in the United States alone are available, and detailed color maps you can zoom in and out of. VZ Navigator is for the United States only, while Global is worldwide. VZ Navigator also incorporates weather and traffic, when applicable.
- **Ringback Tones**   A ringback tone is what callers hear when they phone you, prior to you answering their call or it being sent to voice mail. This is not the same thing as a ring tone, which is what you hear when people call you. You get to choose the song each of your contacts hear, and a song can be applied to a single person or a group of contacts. You can even incorporate Jukebox, which will randomly select a song for each call that arrives.
- **V CAST Music**   A music service that allows you to preview, purchase, and download music to your phone from the V CAST Music catalog. You can also get music using your PC and free Rhapsody software. You can manage your music library, create playlists, and transfer compatible music easily.

To access information about these services to learn more about them:

1. Visit www.verizon.com.
2. Create a user name and password.
3. Log in.
4. On the Home tab, under Quick Links, click Add/Change Features.
5. At the bottom of the page, click *available features*.
6. Click any service to learn more about it. I suggest VZ Navigator.
7. Click Back to Services.
8. Click V CAST Music.
9. Click Back to Services.
10. Click Ringback Tones.

Install and Use VZ Navigator

If VZ Navigator seems like something you'd like to try, you'll need to download and install it. Luckily, a link is available in the Application Center on your BlackBerry Storm2. After VZ Navigator has been installed, and you've agreed to the additional fee, you'll be ready to use the application. VZ Navigator is $9.99 a month, or you can opt to use VZ Navigator for a 24-hour period for $2.99.

FIGURE 17-2   VZ Navigator is probably not yet installed.

To download and install VZ Navigator:

    Installing VZ Navigator Global is almost the same as installing VZ Navigator.

1. From the BlackBerry Menu screen, click Application Center.
2. Locate VZ Navigator. If it shows it is not installed (see Figure 17-2), click to start the installation process.
3. Click Install, and then click I Agree to the terms of service.
4. Click Download VZ Navigator. Click Download again to start.
5. If prompted, give the application "Trusted Status."
6. Click OK, and click the End button on the phone.

You must now confirm that the BlackBerry Storm2's GPS Services feature is on. By default, GPS is set to provide GPS information only when dialing 911. To turn on location services for VZ Navigator:

1. From the BlackBerry Menu screen, click Options.
2. Click Advanced Options.
3. Click GPS.
4. Set GPS Services to Location On.

Start VZ Navigator

The first time you start VZ Navigator, you'll have to perform a few setup tasks, including reviewing application settings, accepting the terms of service, and agreeing to pay the monthly fee for the service. You'll also need to wait while data downloads, including voices, weather information, and maps.

To start and configure VZ Navigator:

1. From the BlackBerry Menu screen, click the Downloads folder.

 Tap the VZ Navigator button currently in the Downloads folder, click the Menu button, and opt to move the application icon to the BlackBerry Home or Menu screen, if you know you'll use it often.

2. Click VZ Navigator to start it.
3. If prompted regarding application control permissions:
   a. Click View.
   b. Review the settings.
   c. Click the Escape key.
   d. Click Save.
4. Read the Terms of Service and click Accept to continue.
5. When prompted to choose to buy the service or decline it, you must click Buy to continue. If you press Decline, you will not be charged and VZ Navigator will close.
6. After pressing Buy, click Accept.
7. Wait while the application downloads. VZ Navigator should start now, and you should be able to view the screen shown in Figure 17-3.

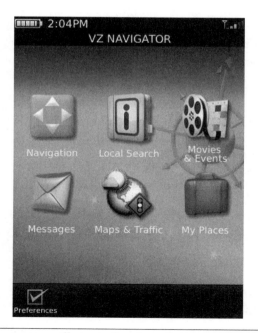

FIGURE 17-3   VZ Navigator will start after installation and agreeing to terms of service and additional monthly fees.

VZ Navigator has six icons on its Home screen:

- **Navigation** Click Navigation to access your recent searches, to view a list of favorites you've input, to view your BlackBerry Storm2 address book (and use an address in it to get directions), to input a new address to navigate to or save, to input your home and work addresses, to locate an airport, or to input an intersection. Once you've decided on a location to navigate to, voice-activated instructions will automatically begin.
- **Local Search** Click Local Search to type what you're looking for (optional), a category for the search (such as eating and drinking, ATMs, movie theaters, hotels and motels, and more), and the location from which you'd like to start the search. You can choose from your current GPS location (which your BlackBerry Storm2 will discover on its own), or choose an address from a variety of places, like an airport, your BlackBerry Storm2 address book, or something that's "in your direction."
- **Movies and Events** Use this feature to access options including Now Playing, Movie Search, Movie Theaters, Events Near Me, Event Search, and Event Venues. Each option enables you to type or choose what you want to see, where you want to see it, the genre you're looking for, the event type, and more. Event types include concerts, dancing and night life, exhibits and art shows, special events, and more. Once you've decided on a particular event and location, click Navigate to get directions.
- **Messages** Use this icon to send and receive messages related to your current GPS location, or a variety of other locations, including but not limited to an address in your address book, any favorite you've saved, an airport, or an intersection. This feature makes it easy to share information with others, such as the address of a movie theater, your home or work address, or a place you'd like to meet. You can also easily send your current GPS location should you ever need help or be lost.
- **Maps and Traffic** Use this icon to get a map of a specific location, find out exactly where you are on a map, to track your current progress on a map, to view traffic, or to get the weather. As with other options, once you've found a place to go, click Navigate for directions. See Figure 17-4.
- **My Places** Use this icon to view addresses and places you've saved and your recent searches. Once you've decided on a location, click Navigate to get there.

 Note VZ Navigator 5.0 was recently released and is available for the BlackBerry Storm2. It offers some new features like the ability to send your location to a dispatcher for roadside assistance, Facebook integration, and new graphics for tunnels, U-turns, and so on.

Find a Route with VZ Navigator

If you've used a GPS navigation system before, you won't have any trouble adjusting to VZ Navigator. It looks and acts like most GPS systems you've used. You locate a place to go, and you click Navigate for turn-by-turn voice directions. If you just want

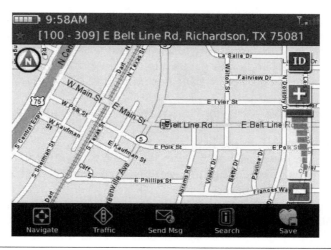

FIGURE 17-4   Navigate is always an option after you find a place you'd like to go.

a map, click Map. If you've never used a GPS system before, don't worry; it's very intuitive. The best place to start is the Navigation icon.

To get directions (find a route) from where you currently are to an address where you'd like to go:

1. Open VZ Navigator.
2. Click Navigation.
3. Click Address.
4. Type the address you want to navigate to.
5. Click the Map icon on the screen to view a map of the address; click Navigate to start turn-by-turn directions.
6. Note the options, shown in Figure 17-5, to save the map, send the map, view traffic, or navigate.

Do More with VZ Navigator

If you read the earlier bulleted list carefully, you know there are many ways you can use VZ Navigator other than to get from point A to point B. Here are some examples: You can send a map of a place to a friend. You can detour around a specific road or traffic.

FIGURE 17-5   VZ Navigator offers options to navigate, save, send a message, and more, once you've decided on an address or location.

You can search for gas stations close to your present location and get their current gas prices. And you can easily search for movies that are playing in movie theaters near your location. The easiest way to learn about what's available is to play around with the various icons and enter data. Here are some things to try:

Find a movie playing in a theater near you:

1. From the VZ Navigator Home screen, click Movies and Events.
2. Click Now Playing.
3. Click a movie in the list.
4. Click Showtimes.
5. Review the showtimes for each theater in your area, and click the entry for the venue to learn more.
6. Click Navigate for turn-by-turn directions or Map to view a map of the area.
7. Click Send Msg to send the information to a friend.
8. To return to the Home screen, click the Back button a few times.

Tip   To send a message, add a recipient and type a message. The information about the location you've found is already included. The information, if it's about a movie, will only include the movie theater location but not the showtimes.

To get a list of gas stations near you and choose the one with the least expensive gas (and navigate there):

1. From the VZ Navigator Home screen, click the Category line. An arrow will appear and options will be presented.
2. Click Gas Stations/Prices.
3. Click Find.
4. Locate the desired gas station. Click Navigate. See Figure 17-6.

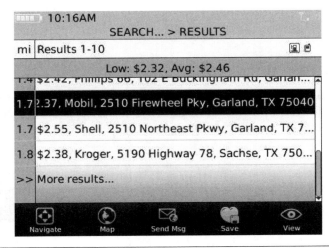

FIGURE 17-6   It's easy to find a nearby gas station, but the perk is that you can review the prices before you go.

Tip Click the Escape button to return to the Home screen.

Lost? Find out where you are with Maps and Traffic:

1. From the VZ Navigator Home screen, click Maps and Traffic.
2. Click Where Am I?
3. If you need help, click Send Msg and type your message.

Tip If you are at a location and want to save that location quickly, click Where Am I?, and then click Save.

Although there are many ways to get the weather, you can get the weather for any location from VZ Navigator. This is especially convenient if you've already saved, say, a particular airport and want to see what the weather's like there before you arrive.
To obtain the weather for a particular airport:

1. From the VZ Navigator Home screen, click Maps and Traffic.
2. Click Weather.
3. Scroll down to Airport and click it.
4. Select your airport from the list (or begin typing the airport name and click it if it appears).
5. The weather report appears, shown in Figure 17-7. Click View to get more information.

Tip When a keyboard is present, you will have to hide the keyboard to view the available icons underneath. Use a downward swipe to remove it (and an upward swipe to show it).

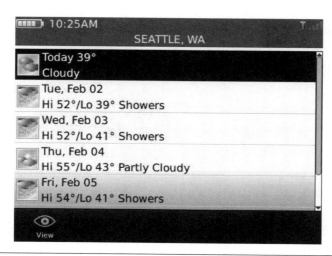

FIGURE 17-7 Get the weather for the location you'll be navigating to.

Sometimes you just don't know what you want. A restaurant, but what's close? Perhaps you need to find a police department or hospital, but you don't know where one is. Maybe you're in desperate need of an ATM, a parking lot, or a Verizon Wireless store. You'll use the Local Search option for these things.

To find something near your current location, including police stations, hospitals, ATMs, parking lots, and more:

1. From the VZ Navigator Home screen, click Local Search.
2. Tap All Categories under Categories and click the arrow that appears.
3. Locate the desired category and click it, and then click the appropriate subcategory.
4. Click Find.

Use Ringback Tones

Ringback tones are just about the least expensive add-on service you can opt for. The Ringback Tones service is $0.99 a month, with a fee of $1.99 per ringtone each year. The charge for this will appear on your bill once you've signed up for the service and purchased a specific ringback tone. Ringback tones are best purchased through the Ringback Tones web site, and must be managed using a home computer, so make sure you have a computer available.

To get started with ringback tones:

1. From the BlackBerry Menu screen, click SMS and MMS.
2. Click the Menu button and click Compose SMS Text.
3. Click To: and type **728**.
4. In the message, type **rbt list**.
5. Read the message you receive in return, shown in Figure 17-8, and type **y** to agree and sign up.

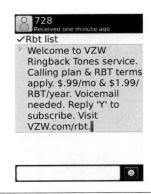

FIGURE 17-8 Send a text message to 728 and type rbt list to get started with Ringback Tones.

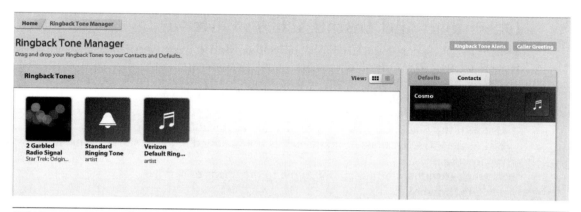

FIGURE 17-9 Apply any ringback tone you have to any contact. Note that, as shown here, there are two generic ringback tones available plus any you've purchased.

To browse Ringback Tones and select one:

1. From a desktop computer, visit www.mediastore.verizonwireless.com. Sign in with your Verizon user name and password.
2. Click the Ringback Tones tab.
3. Locate a ringback tone to buy.
4. Click Buy Ringback Tone, agree to the terms and conditions, and click Checkout.
5. Read the information in the resulting window and click OK. (Remain logged in to the site.)

To assign a ringback tone to a contact:

1. While still logged in to the Media Store, click Manage at the top of the page.
2. Click My Ringback Tones.
3. Click New Contact.
4. Type the contact's name and phone number.
5. Drag the icon for the ringback tone you want to apply to the contact. See Figure 17-9.
6. Repeat as desired.

Use V CAST Music

V CAST Music | Rhapsody is a music option available to you from your BlackBerry Storm2. As noted, you can use this application and the Verizon Media store to obtain music you want and manage it. However, you'll have to pay for the media you access as you do with other add-on media services, so if you already have a music preference, like iTunes or your own personal music library, you may not need a service like this one.

Download and Install V CAST Music

As with VZ Navigator, you'll need to install and download the V CAST Music software, agree to some terms and conditions, and allow the application to work with your phone. Rhapsody is free, but you have to purchase songs. Songs range in price, generally from $0.99 to $1.99 per song. There is no monthly fee for V CAST Music.

1. From the BlackBerry Menu screen, click Application Center.
2. Locate V CAST Music. If it shows it is not installed, click to start the installation process.
3. Click Install, and then click I Agree to the terms of service.
4. Click Download.

 If the screen goes dark and you want to view the download process, click the Menu button on the phone.

5. Reboot the phone, as prompted.

 Having trouble finding V CAST Music on your phone after you've done the preceding steps? You won't find it in the Downloads folder, and there won't be an icon for it on your screen, but check out the Media folder under Music. There it sits! So, in the Media folder, click Go To V CAST Music | Rhapsody.

Now you'll need to locate the V CAST Music | Rhapsody application and perform a few setup tasks:

1. On the BlackBerry Menu screen, click Media.
2. Click Music.
3. Click Go To V CAST Music | Rhapsody. See Figure 17-10.
4. Click Do Not Ask Again and click Allow.
5. Click OK. Once you're in, you're ready to browse the music available at the V CAST Music | Rhapsody store.

Download a Song with V CAST Music

Inside the V CAST Music | Rhapsody application, you can search, look at what's new, review features of the program, and more. Once you've found a song you like, simply click Buy.

To browse for, buy, and download a song:

1. From the BlackBerry Menu screen, click Media.
2. Click Music.
3. Click Go To V CAST Music | Rhapsody.

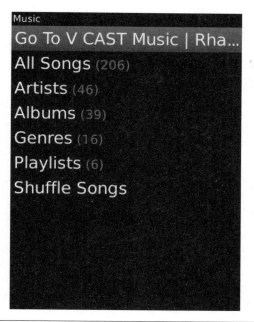

FIGURE 17-10   You'll find access to V CAST Music and Rhapsody from the Music folder.

4. Browse the store using these options:
   a. What's New
   b. What's Hot
   c. Features
   d. Recommended
   e. Browse

Note   Download, an option on the V CAST Music | Rhapsody Home screen, lists songs you've purchased but not yet downloaded.

5. After you've found a song to buy, click Buy.
6. Click Buy This Song to verify your choice.
7. Click Download Now.
8. Choose where you want the song to be saved (choose Memory Card).
9. Download the song now.

PART V

Appendixes

A

BlackBerry Tips and Tricks

Knowing shortcuts for using your BlackBerry Storm2 allows you to perform tasks more quickly than you could otherwise. Shortcuts also allow you to be more productive and less frustrated when performing a job. Did you know you can, while in a keyboard, hold down the "number" key for a second or so, and then, for as long as you want, keep the number pad on the screen? That's a pretty cool feature, especially if you're trying to type a phone number in an instant message. If you didn't know that trick, to type in a phone number you'd have to click a number (after which the regular keyboard would reappear), click the number key again to bring back the number pad, click another number, click the number key again to bring back the number pad, and well, you get the idea. This happens because by default, after you press a number on the number pad, the alphabet keys automatically appear and the number keys go away. This same trick applies to the sym key, caps key, and others.

In this appendix, you'll learn several shortcuts like this one. This can help you save time, and can be quite enlightening. Keep in mind that a few of these tricks and tips are also scattered throughout the book, but having a reference here is certainly in order. Most of the information is new, though, and warrants a good look. The tips are listed alphabetically, to assist in finding them quickly.

Add an Entry to the Custom Dictionary

Do you use words that your BlackBerry doesn't recognize, like a company name, product name, or other word? If so, add that word to the Custom Dictionary, and it'll always be recognized by your phone when you type it. Click Options, Custom Dictionary, and then click the Menu button and New to add an entry.

Auto On and Off (Turn Your Phone On and Off Automatically)

You can configure when you want your BlackBerry Storm2 to be active. The Auto On/ Off feature lets you disable your phone during certain times of the day or night, or on weekends. Click Options, Auto On/Off, and for Weekday or Weekend, change Disabled to Enabled. Configure the times as desired. Save the changes.

Auto Text (Define Your Own Shortcuts)

If there's something you have to type a lot, perhaps a person's name, a company name, or even a phrase like, "I'm going to the gym now and won't have my phone with me," you can add a shortcut to it in the AutoText options. Click Options, click AutoText, click the Menu button, and click New. Under Replace, type a shortcut for the word or phrase you want to create a shortcut for, such as your initials for your entire name, or GTG for "going to the gym." Then fill in the With field with the text you'd like to replace your shortcut with, such as your name or a phrase. Click the Menu button and click Save.

Backlighting (Turn On)

To turn on backlighting, perhaps to view the cover art for a song that's playing or to show the light after it's faded out, press the Power button.

Bedside Mode (Enable)

To enable Bedside mode, which will keep your phone quiet while you sleep, click the Clock icon, and click the screen once the clock appears. Click Enter Bedside Mode.

Block Your Phone Number when Making a Call

If you need to call someone but don't want to reveal your number, you can restrict your identity with a few clicks. Click Options, General Options, and in Restrict My Identity, click Always.

Browse the Internet Faster

When you're able to use Wi-Fi and 3G is enabled for Internet browsing, you can browse more quickly if you change the Browser Configuration settings. Open the

FIGURE A-1   Choose the Hotspot Browser for faster Internet browsing.

Browser, click the Menu button, and click Options. Click Browser Configuration, and for Browser, choose Hotspot Browser, shown in Figure A-1.

Capitalize a Letter

To capitalize any letter, press the caps key on the keyboard once, and then type the letter. You can also press and hold the letter on the keyboard until the capitalized letter appears.

Change the Sound Profile

If you need to change your sound profile often, consider moving the Sounds icon to the BlackBerry Home screen and into the top eight spots. Then, click the Sounds icon to change your profile quickly.

Change the Phone List View to "Most Used"

Click Options, click Phone Options, and then click General Options. Change Phone List View to Most Used. This will change the Call Log to show the most used numbers at the top of the list and the least used at the bottom. The Call Log will no longer show calls by date and time.

Change the Theme

You can download themes that make changes to your phone sounds, wallpaper, icons, and convenience keys. If you download and install a theme, it will probably be applied automatically. If you're ready to change themes, though, perhaps to return to a previously used theme, click Options, click Theme, and then select the theme to use from the list.

Check for Updates

Occasionally there will be wireless updates available for your phone. You can check for these updates manually. Click Options, Advanced Options, and Wireless Updates to get started.

Copy Text

To copy text, you first have to highlight it. (See the "Highlight Text" section.) Once the text is highlighted, you'll see the options Cut, Copy, Cancel Selection (and perhaps others) at the bottom of the screen. Click Copy to copy the text. Later you can paste it. See Figure A-2.

Customize the Convenience Buttons

If there's an application you use often, assign a convenience button to it. You'll be able to access the application with a single click. Click Options, click Screen/Keyboard, and then select the desired application for Rich Side Convenience Key Opens and Left Side Convenience Key Opens. Save the changes.

Cut Text

To cut text, you first have to highlight it. (See the "Highlight Text" section.) Once the text is highlighted, you'll see the options Cut, Copy, Cancel Selection (and perhaps others) at the bottom of the screen. Click Cut to copy the text. Later you can paste it.

FIGURE A-2   After you've highlighted text, these controls will appear at the bottom of the screen.

Delete Data on Your Memory Card

You can fill up a memory card pretty quickly if you store a lot of data on your BlackBerry. If you think the card is getting full, either connect the phone to your computer and move the data off it, or delete some of the data stored on the phone. There are several areas where you'll find data:

- **Media**   Be especially vigilant to delete unwanted videos, pictures, and music.
- **Downloads**   Make sure to delete downloads for applications you no longer use.
- **Messages**   Don't let messages pile up, especially if they include memory-hogging attachments.

Delete Multiple Messages

To delete multiple messages at once, touch the first message in the list to delete, and then touch the last message in the list to delete. Press the Delete button that appears on the screen. If you need to select more, scroll down and touch the screen again. You can select multiple messages this way. See Figure A-3.

Every message list includes various headers to separate the messages you receive by the date they were received. Touch any date header, click the Menu key, and click Delete Prior to delete all messages prior to that date.

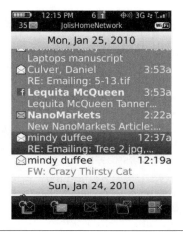

FIGURE A-3   Select multiple e-mails for the option to delete them all with a single click.

Edit Text

To edit text you've written (this does not include text someone else has written in an e-mail or message you're forwarding), click where you'd like to start editing. Hold that click a second or so, and a cursor will appear. You can then use your finger to slide the cursor to the area of the text you'd like to edit. Use the back arrow to erase letters.

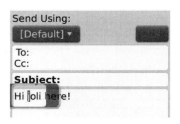

Exit Anything

To exit any dialog box, window, application, or other item, click the Escape key.

Extend Battery Life

There are several ways to extend how long your phone can run on a single battery charge:

- *Turn off GPS when you aren't using it.*   Click Options, Advanced Options, GPS, and set GPS Services to E911 only.
- *Change mobile network to 1xEV instead of Global.*   Click Options, Mobile Network, and change Network Technology to 1XEV instead of Global (unless you need global access, that is).
- *Turn off Wi-Fi when you aren't using it.*   Click the bars on the BlackBerry Home screen, located in the top-right corner. Deselect Wi-Fi by clicking it once.
- *Turn off Bluetooth when you aren't using it.*   Click the bars on the BlackBerry Home screen, located in the top-right corner. Deselect Bluetooth by clicking it once.
- *Reduce the brightness of the screen.*   Click Options, Screen/Keyboard, and change levels as desired. Note there is Backlight Timeout, Automatically Dim Backlight, and Backlight Brightness.
- *Delete apps you don't use.*   Click Options, click Applications, and touch an application to uninstall. Click Delete on the screen. Click Delete again to verify.
- *Disable message notifications.*   Click the Sounds icon and choose Edit Profiles. Disable sounds as applicable.

Focus in on a Subject Before Taking a Picture

Click the right convenience key to focus in on a subject before taking the picture. When you're ready, use the same key to take the photo.

Get Help

There's a Help icon on your phone that enables you to browse the most common help-related issues Verizon and BlackBerry know about. There are Help files on just about anything imaginable, sorted by topic. There are several topics you may be interested in now:

- Shortcuts
- Voice commands
- Messages
- Typing
- Search
- Display and keyboard
- Browser
- Bluetooth
- Wi-Fi technology
- Power, battery, and memory

Hide Any Icon on the BlackBerry Home Screen

Remove icons you don't use from your BlackBerry Home screen to minimize what you have to browse to locate the icon you want to use. Touch any icon you'd like to hide, click the Menu button on the phone, and then click Hide.

Hide the Keyboard

Sometimes the keyboard is just in the way. You can hide the keyboard by swiping downward with your finger, starting just above the keyboard on the screen.

Highlight Text

To highlight text, press with your left thumb where the text you'd like to highlight starts, and while holding down that thumb, press with the other thumb where the text to highlight stops. See Figure A-4.

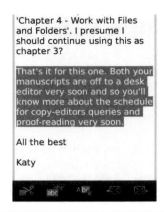

'Chapter 4 - Work with Files
and Folders'. I presume I
should continue using this as
chapter 3?

That's it for this one. Both your
manuscripts are off to a desk
editor very soon and so you'll
know more about the schedule
for copy-editors queries and
proof-reading very soon.

All the best

Katy

FIGURE A-4 Highlighted text

Insert a Period

To quickly insert a period, click the Space key twice. A period will be inserted and the first letter of the next sentence will be capitalized.

Insert the @ Symbol

If you don't know this trick, by now you're probably pretty annoyed at the number of keystrokes required to insert an @ symbol when you're inside an e-mail field. Here it is: Press the space key.

Install a Verizon Application Such as VZ Navigator or V CAST Music

The Verizon applications you want are already on your phone. To find them and install them, click the Application Center icon. Then, locate the application to install, click Install, and follow any additional prompts.

Log All Calls

By default, only missed calls appear in the Call Log. You can log all calls if desired. Click Options, click Phone Options, and then click Call Logging. Click All Calls and save changes.

Move an Icon from One Area of the Home Screen to Another

The icons you see on your BlackBerry Home screen probably aren't optimized for your use. Consider moving the eight icons you use most to the top eight fields on your BlackBerry screen. Consider Messages, SMS and Text, Sounds, Media, Lock, Maps, My Verizon, and Search, for instance. To move an icon, touch the icon to move, and click the Menu button on the phone. Click Move. Tap another area of the screen to move the icon there. Click the Menu button again and click Complete Move.

Move to Another Item in a List

To move to another item in a list, slide your finger to the left or the right quickly.

Multitap (Enable)

If you prefer multitap over other keyboard options, in any keyboard view, click the Menu key and click Enable Multitap.

Mute a Song

When playing a song, you can use the volume buttons on the right side of the phone to adjust the volume. You may not know that you can also mute a song quickly by pressing a button on the top of the phone. Press the button on the top-right part of the phone, to the right of the Power button to mute any song.

Pan

To pan in a picture, slide your finger in any direction.

Password-Protect Your Phone

When you password-protect your phone, you have to enter the password each time you want to use the phone. While this can be annoying to you, it would certainly thwart a would-be thief. To apply a password, click Options and Password. And change the Password field to Enabled. Then click Set Password and follow the prompts.

Paste Text

To paste text, you first have to highlight it (see the "Highlight Text" section) and cut or copy it (see the "Copy Text" and "Cut Text" sections). Once the text has been copied or cut, open a message or some other application where you'd like to text it. Then, click the Menu button on the phone, and click Paste from the options that appear. The text will be pasted.

Phone View

When you click the green Call button on your phone, the Phone application opens. What you see when it opens is the same view as was selected the last time you made a call. If you prefer to always have the Phone application open in a specific view, such as Dial Pad, Contact List, or Call Log, you can apply that setting in Phone Options. In the Phone application, click the Menu key. Click Options. Click General Options. For Initial View, select Dial Pad, Call Log, Contacts, or Previous. Save the changes.

Play the Next Song in a List Using the Volume Keys

There are several ways to move from song to song in a list, but did you know you can use the Volume keys too? Instead of clicking up or down quickly with those keys, as you would to change the volume, hold down the key for a second instead. This action will cause the media player to skip to the next song in the list.

Remove an E-mail Account from Your Phone

If you've added several e-mail accounts to your BlackBerry, but have now decided you don't need to receive mail from them on your BlackBerry, you can delete them. Unfortunately, deleting an account from your phone is nearly impossible. The best way to remove an e-mail account on your BlackBerry is to do so from the BlackBerry Internet Service web site, using a desktop or laptop computer (see Figure A-5). Locating and signing in to this site is outlined in Chapter 7. Once you're on the site, click Email Accounts. Click Delete for the account you want to stop receiving mail from.

FIGURE A-5 It's best to manage e-mail accounts on the BlackBerry Internet Service web site.

Save a Picture You Find on the Web

Browse to the actual picture you'd like to save. Click the Menu button and click Save Image. Accept the current name of the image or type another. Click Save. Note you can also save this picture as wallpaper.

Scroll

To scroll down, slide your finger upward on the screen. Perform this action quickly to scroll quickly. To scroll up, slide your finger downward on the screen. Perform this action quickly to scroll quickly.

Search Calendars for a Keyword

To search your calendars for a keyword, click Search on the BlackBerry screen. Tick Calendar, untick Messages, and type the text to search for. All instances of that keyword found in your calendars will appear.

Search Messages for a Keyword

To search all existing messages for a keyword, click the Search icon. Then type the keyword to search for and click the magnifying glass. All messages with that keyword will appear in a list.

Select a Running Application

From the Home screen, click the Menu key and hold it for a second or two. The App Switcher will appear where you can quickly select any running application.

Separate E-mail and SMS in the Messages List (or Combine Them)

In your Messages list you may see only e-mail messages, or you may see both e-mail and SMS messages. You can choose which of these options you prefer under Options, General Options. The setting is SMS and Email Inboxes. You can choose Combined or Separate or, if you have a theme applied, Theme Controlled. If you only want to view e-mails here, or if you prefer to see both e-mail and SMS, make that change under Options.

Set Song as Ringtone

Locate the song in Media, Music, and touch the song to select it. Click the Menu key and click Set as Ringtone.

Show Keyboard Quickly

To show the keyboard, swipe your finger quickly from the bottom of the screen upward.

Show Status Screen Quickly

To view the phone's status, including but not limited to phone number, device MEIDhex, Device BlackBerry PIN, language list, model number, Hardware Version, and PRL Version, from the keypad dial #4357*.

Sort Contacts by First Name, Last Name, or Company

By default your contacts appear in the Contact list sorted by their first names. This is easy to change. Click the Contacts icon, click the Menu button, and click Options. In the Contacts Options, next to Sort By, select your sorting option.

Sort Messages to Show Only Those from a Specific Contact

To view messages from a single contact, together sorted by their date, locate a message from the contact in the Messages list. Then, touch and gently hold that touch on the contact name and wait for the list to be sorted and reappear.

Speed Dialing (Configure a Speed Dial Number)

To configure a speed dial number so that you only need press and hold one number on the Dial Pad to place a call to that number, click Options, click Phone Options, and click Speed Dial Numbers. Click a speed dial entry that is blank and select the contact to apply to that number from the resulting contact list.

SureType (Enable)

If you prefer SureType over other keyboard options, in any keyboard view, click the Menu key and click Enable SureType.

Switch to Another Program

If you are in one program but need to switch to another, you don't have to press the Escape key to return to the BlackBerry Home screen. Instead, click the Menu key and click Switch Application. Select the running application to switch to.

Take Better Pictures

When you're in the Camera application, click the Menu button and click Options. There, configure the settings for the pictures you take. These include but are not limited to:

- **Autofocus**   Choose from Normal or Close Up for best results.
- **Image stabilization**   Leave this setting on Yes to reduce the incidence of blurry images.
- **Picture Quality**   Choose from Superfine, Fine, and Normal. See what works best for the images you take.

Type a Special Character

To type a special character or to see what special characters are available with this technique, open an application that allows you to type. Gently touch any key and wait for a second while the special characters appear above it. If you see a character you like, click it. There are lots of characters; for instance, over the M on the keyboard (after you touch and hold it, that is), is the option to insert three dots (...). Touch the A S key to view all of the options for the letter "a" including an "a" with all kinds of accent marks.

View Your Usage Data

Sign up for My Verizon (visit www.verizon.com) and download the My Verizon app. Click it to view update usage information including:

- **Balance**   To view the balance due on your account.
- **Usage**   To view usage information including minutes, messaging, and data.

- **Payment**   To make a payment using your phone, to view your last five payments, to edit your payment accounts, to request a copy of your latest bill, and more.
- **My Plan**   To view your current plan and features. This can include caller ID, call waiting, call forwarding, night and weekend minutes, e-mail and web, and more.
- **My Features**   To view your current features, which can include e-mail and web, Roadside Assistance, blocking features, and features unique to Verizon, outlined in Chapter 16.
- **Vmail Pswd**   To change your voicemail password.
- **My Services**   To view your services including family locator and the like, or to access service options, such as finding a store nearby or updating your billing address.
- **Mobile2Mobile**   To join or view your mobile to mobile calling plan, and to check to see if numbers you call often are part of your mobile network.
- **FAQs**   To view frequently asked questions and their answers related to billing, voice mail, roaming and traveling, and more.

Visual Voice Mail

If you have a few extra dollars a month to spend, consider Visual Voice Mail. With this feature you no longer have to dial your voice mail account to hear your voice mails. They are stored on your phone as they arrive. To hear your voice mails, you simply click Visual Voice Mail, click the voice mail to hear, and listen! You can also delete your voice mails easily from the same interface; click Callback, or even Reply.

Voicemail Password (Have It Entered Automatically when You Check Your Voicemail)

When you check your voicemail, you have to enter a password. You can bypass this step by saving your password in the Voicemail options settings. To enter your voicemail password, click the green call button, click the Menu button, and then click Options. Click Voice Mail. Input your password. Click the Menu button again to save your changes.

Zoom in on a Web Page or Picture

To zoom in to a picture or web page, touch the screen quickly two times. To zoom out, press the Escape key. You can also access zoom features in some screens from the bottom of the screen, shown in Figure A-6.

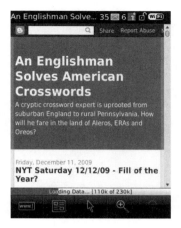

FIGURE A-6   You can zoom in on a web page using a double-tap on the screen.

Zoom in on a Subject While Using the Camera

You can use the volume keys to zoom in and out of a subject while using the camera. Press the up key to zoom in, and the down key to zoom out.

B

Backup, Restore, Reset, and Troubleshoot

HOW TO...

- Back up your BlackBerry data
- Schedule automatic backups
- Restore BlackBerry data
- Erase your personal data
- Find information on the Internet
- Explore the BlackBerry's Owner's Lounge

You may never have any problems with your BlackBerry, but that doesn't mean you shouldn't back up the data on it. Even if you never encounter a manufacturer-related problem, you may accidentally drop the phone or spill something on it, making it unusable. Worse, the phone could be lost or stolen. In any case, it's best to always have a backup, for the same reason you carry health, life, and car insurance. Just in case.

You perform all backup tasks from the BlackBerry Desktop Manager on your computer. You installed this software when you installed the CD that came with your phone. If you haven't installed that software yet, do so now. If you've misplaced the software CD since then, you can also download the Desktop Software from BlackBerry web site (http://na.blackberry.com/eng/services/desktop/desktop_pc.jsp). Once the software has been installed, you'll see the Backup and Restore option from the Main menu.

Back Up Your BlackBerry Data and Schedule Automatic Backups

You should back up your phone regularly, and store the backup on your computer. If you ever require it to restore your phone, the data will be readily available. If your data is extremely sensitive or enormously important, consider backing up your phone to an online server or a computer at work. There's always the possibility that the disaster that destroys your BlackBerry also destroys your computer (broken water heater, fire, tornado).

To back up your BlackBerry to your computer using the BlackBerry Desktop Manager and to create a backup schedule:

1. At your computer, connect your BlackBerry using the USB cable and start the BlackBerry Desktop Manager.
2. On the Main menu page, click Backup and Restore.
3. Under Backup, click Options. In the Options window:
   a. Tick "Back up on-board device memory."
   b. If desired, tick "Encrypt backup file."
   c. Tick "Back up my device automatically every ____ days."
   d. Accept the default setting to back up all device application data.
   e. Click OK.
4. Back at the Backup and Restore window, click Backup.

 If you're using a laptop for backing up your phone, make sure it's plugged in or has enough battery power to complete the task.

5. Browse to a location to save the backup file, name the file, and click Save. It's best to keep the defaults if you can; the software will know exactly where to look if you ever need to restore the data.
6. If prompted that Mass Storage Mode is not enabled, click OK to enable it.
7. Wait while the backup completes.

Restore BlackBerry Data

Hopefully, you'll never need to restore the data you've backed up, but if you do, it's a pretty easy process. Remember, though, you'll be restoring from your last backup and if that backup was six months ago, well, that's all you'll have to restore. With any luck, you've followed the advice here to back up your device once a week. You can't lose much in a week!

That said, here's how to restore data should you ever need to:

1. At your computer, connect your BlackBerry and start the BlackBerry Desktop Manager.
2. On the Main menu page, click Backup and Restore.
3. Under Restore, click Restore.
4. Browse to the location of your most recent backup and click it. See Figure B-1.
5. Click Open, if applicable.
6. When prompted, click Yes to start the restore process.

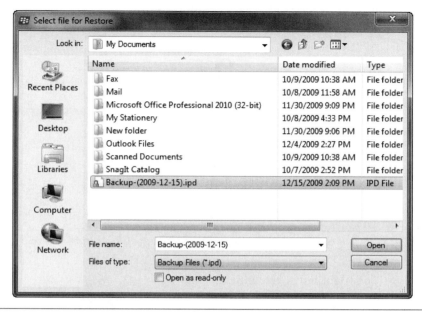

FIGURE B-1   Locate your most recent backup, select it, and click Open.

Erase Your Personal Data

If you ever want to sell your BlackBerry Storm2 or give it to a family member or friend, you'll want to erase all your personal data. When wiping out all of your personal data, you'll delete the following (which will be erased and gone forever if no backup exists):

- Pictures
- Music
- Videos
- Ring tones
- Applications
- Network information
- E-mail settings, e-mails, contacts, and so on
- Anything on your media card

To erase all of the personal data on your BlackBerry Storm2:

1. On the BlackBerry menu screen, click Options.
2. Click Security Options.
3. Click Security Wipe.
4. Select all options shown in Figure B-2:
   a. Emails, Contacts, and so on
   b. User Installed Application
   c. Media Card

FIGURE B-2 Select what data to wipe. Select each option to remove all personal data.

5. Type **blackberry** to confirm.
6. Click Wipe.

Find Information on the Internet

You can obtain help and support from many web sites on the Internet. If you need to troubleshoot a problem that backing up and restoring won't fix, this is the way to go. There are many sites you can visit including:

- **BlackBerry**   Visit www.blackberry.com to visit the official BlackBerry web site. There you can access additional pages to learn where to buy a BlackBerry (they may be able to help you resolve a problem) or sign up to visit the BlackBerry Owner's Lounge. At the Owner's Lounge, you can often resolve technical problems quickly, from subpages entitled Tips and Tricks, Downloads, and Useful Information.
- **CrackBerry**   Visit www.crackberry.com to read reviews, post to BlackBerry forums, and chat with other BlackBerry owners. You'll also have access to lots of help pages, "getting started" guides, Help and Discussion forums, and more.
- **BlackBerry Docs**   Visit http://docs.blackberry.com to browse official product documents like user guides, "getting started" guides, and tips and tricks documents.
- **The Official BlackBerry Blog**   Visit http://blogs.blackberry.com to comment on your phone, get help, and read the latest news and reviews. You'll also have access to tips, tricks, and useful guides to help you get more from your phone.
- **Help on your phone**   You can also get help right from your phone. Click Help on the BlackBerry menu screen.

You can type your query or problem into any search engine (such as Google, Bing, or Yahoo!) to search for specific information.

Index

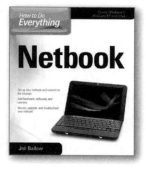